GREAT
GODDESSES

# NIKITA GILL

# GREAT GODDESSES

## Life Lessons from Myths and Monsters

G. P. PUTNAM'S SONS
NEW YORK

*For you,*
*whose iron*
*is as valuable*
*as ichor*

**PUTNAM**
— EST. 1838 —

G. P. PUTNAM'S SONS
*Publishers Since 1838*
An imprint of Penguin Random House LLC
penguinrandomhouse.com

First American edition published by G. P. Putnam's Sons, 2019
First published in 2019 by Ebury Press
Ebury Press is part of the Penguin Random House group of companies

ISBN 9780593085646

Printed in the United States of America
4th Printing

# Contents

# 1. A Mortal Interlude

I lost a God once. It's easier done than people think. Forget a prayer once in a while or simply grow grief in your kitchen window along with the basil and rosemary. Somewhere inside my heart, I misplaced my faith, misunderstood my own origin story, became a person half tragedy, more misery, and I started to relish it. I revelled in this losing of everything that I thought I was, the lack of self-care; the drowning becomes such a needful thing when you think there is nothing left to look forward to. When my faith came back to me, like the forgiving water of a river to the pebbles that it smooths by constant weather and wear, I asked myself, what happens to the Gods when their people forget how to know them? What happens to their fearsome might when the fervent belief fades?

Do you think they are still powerful when they become less than a memory?

Or do you think without the power of prayer everything that makes them immortal is nothing but a façade?

## The Primordial Goddesses

'Verily at the first Khaos (Chaos, the Chasm) [Air] came to be, but next wide-bosomed Gaia (Gaea, Earth), the ever-sure foundations of all the deathless ones who hold the peaks of snowy Olympos ...'

—Hesiod, *Theogony 116*

# Chaos

Edward Lorenz, the mathematician,
father of chaos theory, defines chaos as:

'When the present determines the future,
but the approximate present does not
approximately determine the future.'

Which loosely translated means:

> *No one knows how the consequences*
> *of our actions will truly play out,*
> *and try as we might, we will never*
> *be the masters of our destiny.*

And Chaos, who has been listening, as she
always does to each of her creations,

laughs because what else does the Ancient Being
Who Created Creation do when a small, impatient

primitive species that insists on quantifying everything
tries to quantify the unfathomable by their small terms?

And as she laughs, the cosmos ripples,
And whole galaxies fall apart.

# Eurynome: The Mother of All Things

This is a lesser known story.
It is a genesis entirely woman-whispered
in the shadows when we meet
in secret, plotting escapes
from unwanted marriages or to untangle
darker devil-deemed desires.
They murmur, in the beginning of everything;
from the bones of Chaos, rose a girl
who built the universe, the stars,
the planets, all because she was looking
for a place to dance. And she waltzed
the earth awake and the rhythm of her feet
fermented the stars alive,
the synchronised sorcery of her fingers
brought the solar system to life,
and the flow of her arms looped
around the sun and commanded
him to open his eyes –
But of course, the rest of the tale
is broken too. This is the story told
in hushed tones. It is the version
of the tale they do not want you to know.
After all, what is more powerful
than women who know all about
the blessed fires inside them that grow.

# Chaos to Nyx, Goddess of the Night

You were so strange and vibrant in your ink-black glory, even I, your own mother, did not know how to name you.

Your siblings, their names came easily because none resonated with the vivid silver purity and vibrant green poison of you. You were named eons after your birth because often names become manifestations, but rarely, do manifestations become their names.

So, instead, I chose to let you fly free and ink the universe with the dark shroud you were born in, your screams echoing into a cosmos that did not know how to be ready for your dark requiem, your cries a warning to prepare for what was to come from your birth.

Oh, Nyx, daughter of mine, mother to both violent death and restful sleep, gentle dreams and putrid nightmares, home to all things both terrifying and glorious, patron saint of murderers and lovers alike, I never told you how to inherit the paradox, or how to make it your birthright.

You, who wove stars into your hair as a girl and equally let them freckle your skin, held the moon up as a looking-glass and bewitched existence for eternity.

You, who turns the nightly view of man-made cities instead into the jewelled throats of queens, hiding evil inside your bosom whilst holding sacred in your womb.

You, who turns children's sleep into fairytale lands and knows how to make your brother Hell's innermost sanctum your home.

And yet, lest they forget how to honour the night, they will forever remember that it is from your ribcage they received Hemera and Aether, the miraculous day and the singular light.

## Nyx to Erebus

*Why are passions prettier in the dark?*
I hear mortals ask each other.
*Are demons allowed to fall in love?*
Children ask their mothers.

Yes. We are. Before their very eyes.
When we sweep through their lands,
I wish they could see the tenderness
in the way the darkness takes the night's hand.

# Gaia

And then there was Gaia.

Chaos baptised her spirit first
inside the glory of her own life
giving: Gaia the purest originator,
creator of fragile, fluid things.

Girlhood came to Gaia in the form
of a woodland nymph who spilled
whole forests from her tongue.

She breathed alive the most verdant
of greens and the warmest
of mahoganies and chestnut
in delicate leaf and sturdy bark.

It was Gaia who first pulled a pin
from her hair and carved out
the hills from her own skin.

The deer were her vowels and the
birds were her consonants, she swore
and predators formed; sharks and lions,
animals were her language

before even the notion of language
was invented, this life bringer who expressed
gentler words in lush grass.

Sculpting volcanoes from what
her siblings thought unremarkable,
she showed them how devastating beauty
was constructed from ordinary things.

# A Primordial Love Story

What do you give to Gaia,
the inventor who made the world?

What does she need to
fill her hands that are already

full of bounty beyond
all our wildest dreams?

You make her curious about love.
You ask her if she ever felt an embrace.

You tell her about the wholeness
of a heart that knows

how to beat for itself and another.
You teach her how to

hold molecules and paint them
bold azure and soft cherry blossom,

golds and creams, let them float
upwards into the air high.

You watch her fall in love
as she creates the majestic dome

and names him her perfect mate,
Ouranos the sky.

# Questions for the Daughters of Nyx

Apate, how do you bear it? The broken beat of betrayal
coming from all the countless hearts you let your
deceivers tear to shreds with their lies?

*I remind myself that lies are often truth-shaped.*
*They're only containers you must turn inside out*
*and shake till the truth tumbles out, wide eyed and confused,*
*blinking in a light it never thought it would see.*

Nemesis, does revenge ever tire you? Do the cries you
craft with your scythe ever soften your heart?

*I was born to bring justice.*
*Not to feel pity for those who felt nothing but glee*
*while building palaces*
*out of the tears born from their treachery.*

Keres, do you ever wish for a life free of the violent deaths
you feed upon from the battlefields to the cities?

*Not while people still bring us bodies.*
*Not while there are still corrupt old men*
*sending unknowing boys to their deaths.*
*Not while the truth is a fire everyone sees*
*and no one puts out.*
*Not while there is evil that needs eating yet.*

Clotho, Lachesis, Atropos, does spinning the yarns of fate not tire you? Do your fingers not feel heavy knowing you hold the fates of so many in your hands?

*Does the night ever tire of the darkness?*
*Does the sea ever tire of her own depths?*
*Do the trees ever tire of their roots?*
*Do mortals ever tire of looking for other mortals to call home?*

Oizys, is it hard knowing we only love you through our misery, and never through our happier days?

*Why would you ever believe I want lifelong patrons,*
*when it is my duty to ease people through their heartache*
*and guide them through their pain?*

*It is my duty to help you find*
*the light at the end of each tunnel,*
*for she is my sister, Hemera, the day.*

# 2. A Mortal Interlude

Sometimes I see us do what they tell us not to. The instructions we have had tattooed in parental ink on our minds since birth are hidden for a while under rebellious spirit. We lather our bodies in confidence as warpaint and wear Goddess instead of Girl at our throats. Ignore the salacious tongues inside our heads that threaten us not to be too full, too ferocious. We turn our spines with the height and thickness of oak trees as they were intended to be, leave our hair wild, let ourselves get lost like rivers in forests. Something ancient beckons us, a haunting that we usually ignore for our fear of the unknown.

Sometimes it whispers, you too can bend life at whim like Gaia, write an obituary to the past version of yourself like Nyx, so why don't you try it for a while?

Sometimes I see us unwrap ourselves from mortal and turn primordial, just for a little while, as though inside us a soft meadow of magical moly has suddenly grown.

Sometimes I watch Girl become Goddess and the metamorphosis is more magnificent than anything I have ever known.

*The Titans*

'Set free the Titans who dared to invade the majesty of Jove [Zeus].'

—Seneca, *Hercules Furens 79 ff*

# Gaia's Golden Children

*Motherhood looks exquisite on you,*
declared Ouranos, holding a newborn babe
in his arms, kissing Gaia's fevered brow
covered in that sacred sweat of life-making,

*Look at the wonder that comes from your womb,*
*each one more radiant than the next.*
*You are incapable of creating*
*anything other than masterpieces.*

*It is true*, thought Gaia, a dozen
perfect, golden children now
playing at their feet, in their arms,
ageing both faster and slower than stars.

*Can deities be blessed with eternal happiness,*
she wondered contentedly,
looking at her bright, buoyant family,
*Can anything in existence?*

Perhaps that is where the dark thought
came from, settling behind her forest-laden eyes:
*Would Ouranos still love these children*
*if they were not his version of beautiful?*

And Tragedy, who had seen the future,
whispered in her ear with necessary cruelty,
'*Take your children and run, my love,*
*for my brother Destiny says, he will not.*'

# The Four Stages of a Poisoning

Have you ever watched the sickening of a flawless love? The way it poisons itself and pales what was once pure and pulsating like a crimson clutch of flowers deprived of water, a slow languishing and wilting. How a *what if* can turn itself into the darkest of self-fulfilling prophecies.

I.

It looks like a mother's worries in the middle of the night, the same ones her children and her chosen husband dismiss as irrational. The way Gaia fretted and paced sleepless, each footstep closer to doubt after doubt that had begun to plague her. She was with child again, forever fertile and a giver, and Ouranos insatiable, could not stop taking. He wanted to fill the world with Titan children who looked like they had been forged in gold, who could invent elements and read water and the universe. To Ouranos, piety and family looked like this, and this alone. But inside Gaia's womb there grew something different, something he would not understand.

All she ever wanted was healthy children; it did not matter if they had skin of gold or sand or stone.

II.

It looks like a father who places the weight of the impossible on his wife and children's shoulders. Nothing but perfection will do. Power blurs the lines between father and overlord sometimes. And Ouranos is father to the pristine heavens and all of the skies, and if the skies have never failed him in their beauty, their clouded risings and fallings, then nothing else is allowed to either.

Not even Gaia, his love, his creator, his everything.

III.

It looks like the shattering of every illusion, the pulling apart of smoke and mirrors to reveal the naked truth, where the person you once loved turns into a stranger from one you once knew. Gaia's newest children are different from their Titan brothers and sisters. Far more powerful, but also petrifying to look at. For all her long and painful birthing of them, they are her medal, her reward. Three one-eyed Cyclopes and three hundred-handed, fifty-headed Hecatoncheires. Gaia sees no difference, she dotes on them from the moment they are born. But their father takes a single look at their tiny arms reaching for him and utters words no parent ever should: *You are too hideous to belong in the world of the living, you should live with the dead.* Words so unnatural that once spoken they lead to a splitting of the fabric of the earth, revealing the molten innermost sanctum of hell. He tears each wriggling, crying bundle from their exhausted mother's arms where she still lies bleeding from childbirth, and whilst she screams in shock, in fury, trying to scramble to her feet; he flings their new infants into Tartarus one after the other.

And as the skies grey with the harshest of his storms, he looks at her defeated form coldly, turns on his heel and leaves.

IV.

It looks like something beyond death itself. For the aftermath of an act of such intense cruelty cannot be captured in words. Gaia weeps alone, over what can never be undone, the earth quaking as her swollen body wracks with painful, inconsolable sobs. *I promise you, one day he will pay,* she vows to her screaming, burning children in red, angry Tartarus as she lifts a furious face to the heavens, *one day, the sky will fall.*

Frequently the poisoning looks mortal.

But occasionally it takes on the malevolent face of the divine.

They were so very close to what could have been perfection. Yet their love rotted too, like ripened fruit left for too long in the storms and sunshine.

# The Unloved Ungods: Hecatoncheires

All children are born equally innocent,
but all children are not born equally loved.

Even with a mother who was earth and a father sky,
a meeting between soil below and rain from above,

nothing could save you from being misunderstood.
Your monstrous existence challenged your father's

fragility in the worst way, he paced the night of your birth,
muttering about how he had fathered Titans and Gods

and you, you with your hundred hands, fifty heads,
you were an abomination in his eyes, even as children.

No one ever told him monsters aren't simply born.
Monsters are made by those who nurture them.

So when you reached for him, and he flinched away,
he had decided for you, and your fate was sealed.

Is there a word for when a father destroys his children?
Is there a name for the anguish of a mother who becomes
venom?

You had fifty heads and a hundred hands, you could
barely walk, and he still sentenced you to hell.

No wonder you were angry, no wonder you raised
yourself with rage. And when you got the bones of a
chance

you took the hand of the enemy against your own family,
and learned hatred so well, you taught Gods how to
dance to the songs of hell.

# A Titan Sisterhood

We built an island when we were young.
We hid it away where no one could find it,

Carved it in secret inside the Aegean sea,
whispered it to each other in secret.

While our brothers feuded for kingdoms
with each other, we stole away together,

the six of us walked into the water, which parted
for us so we could stroll along the sea floor.

Tethys found where the salt water met sweet,
and Rhea nurtured the earth until it gave us lilies

and Theia plucked the moon from the sky,
and Phoebe clapped her hands and radiance abounded,

on this island of ours where light was forever.
Listen, this is the way of sisters.

We know how to love each other, we do not need
to speak to know the vastness of emotion between us.

And this is ours, we tell each other fiercely,
Ours and not theirs and we will protect it

from their greedy gazes, so Mnemosyne
is the one who is entrusted with remembering

while Themis charms our minds so we forget.
For this is the only place we are not trembling,

where it does not matter if we are women,
or Goddesses, or Titanides meant to be celestial maps.

Where we find each other by the water,
where we lay our heads in each other's laps.

Where we learn what to call this bond
whilst the palm trees whisper to us,

'Home. Call yourselves "home".'

# What It Means to Be a Forgotten Magic Maker

oracle
/ˈɒrək(ə)l/

*Asteria*
1. When she was born, pale, gleaming, constellations woven through her hair, the cosmos clear in her liquid eyes, her father's gentle prophetic voice blessed her to be the mother of falling stars and nocturnal prophets.
2. There was no warning about how painful it was to tell a star of its own ending, a girlhood spent telling exquisite things, that it is their time to die.
3. The heartache in being Goddess of prophecy meant to be able to read only dark tea leaves in her own divination and still, *still* try to love wholly and without restriction.
4. Wife of the God of destruction, mother to Goddess of necromancy and still, those arrogant Olympians only saw her as spoils of war, as less than even human.
5. They shall not have her, even if they imprison her husband. She handed her daughter over to Styx, asked her to turn her child chthonic, forever make her a being of fear to even ruling Gods like Zeus and Poseidon.

6. The only way to escape them all is to turn herself into something they could never have, her choices: island or constellation.
7. Prophecy told her to transform into an island, for one day, on her banks, her sister will give birth to the sun and the moon.
8. When Olympus falls, and it will, she will be waiting for the last of her family, the last sanctified place left, untouched by Gods and by mortal men.

necromancy
/'nɛkrə(ʊ)mansi/

*Hecate*
1. The inheritance of a lost mother is sometimes soft and sanctified, and sometimes it is loud and litigious and an act of rebellion, and this is why her mother gave her to the underworld.
2. Styx was kind, she showed her how to turn dead waters and dark destinies into resurrections and vivid dreams.
3. She learned her alphabet from ghosts and heard bedtime stories from the decaying throats of the dead, and we all know what this kind of nurture does to a girl.

4. Befriender of runaway nymphs and broken queens of Troy, she guides them into accepting the graceful darkness she wears so easily.
5. When the Gods fail to defeat giants, she smiles softly at Hades: *your mistake is thinking Gods can do a Goddess's job.*
6. She alchemised the amber yellow of an eternal flame and brought down giant after giant with ease that worried Zeus himself.
7. Everyone thinks death is about endings, but it had always been her guide and teacher, her black hounds at her heel in every city she visited, cemetery after cemetery full of ghosts eager to meet her.
8. Does a heart that is rotted cease to be called a heart? Is a mortuary truly just full of dead flesh? Or is it simply waiting for you, Hecate, queen of paradox, of crossroads, to breathe it into second life again.

magic
/ˈmadʒɪk/

*Circe*

1. Did the girl choose magic, or does magic choose the girl? An eternal riddle that circles even the fiercest of the divinities.

2. Perhaps magic is in the habit of choosing sharp-eyed girls who ask too many questions for their own good. Perhaps it chooses girls who are not unloved, but not fully loved either.
3. Or maybe she calls it to her by being immortal, but rejecting her thick, sweet-smelling ichor and naming herself traitor to her kind.
4. Who needs a Sun God's ruthless court of the forever living and bitterly gleaming when one can have an island filled with lions and wolves who adore her for who she is, Goddess of herbs, or poisons, of turning every man who dares step foot here into pigs.
5. Some of us prefer the lonely to the glittering, the shaded hoods of trees to the constant glare of burning ochre.
6. Why be a half-finished poem in some forgotten poet's story, when one can be an odyssey in and of herself, part magic, part villain, part Goddess, part lover.
7. Magic aids her turn from defenceless nymph to Goddess – deathless majesty of a Titanide, summoner of an army of sharks and scorpions alike that would die to protect her.

# The River of the Dead

My father, Oceanus, craved terror,
drifted in and out of the midnight sea.
A shark's mouth became his home
for a while and this is how I was conceived.

He met something on his travels,
something treacherous and odious,
a novelty he had to have, just because
he had had nothing like it before.

When he swam back to Tethys with a baby
my stepmother and sisters recoiled from me.
Sharp blue teeth, yellow-eyed like a fury,
shaped less nymph, more Mormolyce,

they made it clear that whatever I was,
they did not want me. But my father
was enchanted, gave me my own river,
told me I was still Goddess while they

were simply nymphs, refused to let me
hear their whispers of *monster*.
Perhaps he should have. Perhaps
he should have paid attention

to the snakes coiled inside me
waiting to strike, when Zeus asked

for the aid of Titans, this is why
I took his side. Whatever mothered me

had a cast iron womb from hell.
Even Hades knows better than to test me.
For it is my waters that the Gods swear oaths to,
where their eternity or diminishment swells.

I am the reason why Semele burned,
why Phaeton fell, why a God can never
break a pact to another. Some call it madness,
I call it balance: one cannot exist without the other.

People think Achilles lived by my waters.
They are wrong. My waters are what ensured
that he would die. You too will meet me one day.
My name is Styx and I am hatred personified.

# Rhea, Mother to Gods

The birth of a God is a lot
like the birth of a mortal,
except the sweat from our brow is silver
and the blood is gold.

The second way we are different
is that we are given our purpose
when our father holds us, and this
is when our fate is foretold.

His large blue hands blessed
each of my siblings with gifts of prophecy
and intelligence and justice and the power
to control summer's heat and winter's cold.

For me, there was no story.
No divination at his lips.
So my mother taught me
the act of nurture.

'In our home,' she told me gently, 'no one
should ever go hungry. This is your only duty.'
It is why I made sure every bowl was filled
from when I was a little girl as I supposed

it was my purpose to satisfy appetite,
to obediently feed everything that came
to me hungry. I believed I was the Goddess
of Satiation. That this was my only true role.

Now he stands before me. My husband,
my lover, and demands all our infant children,
for his ambition is hungry and only
the blood of our own will quench it.

No one taught me
how to challenge hunger
nor how to deny power.

'Goddess of Satiation,' he goads,
'Goddess of Appetite, isn't
this your only purpose and power?'

So I close my eyes, hold my child out,
and turn away, weeping,
as his greedy mouth devours.

# Leto, Mother to Sun and the Moon

*How do you prevent a God from loving you?*

You learn to veil your beauty through the powers of the oblivion from the magical lotus, take whole meadows and turn them into hiding places, find a secret oasis inside forests to make your own – you have learned early, and wisely, that even the daughters of Titans do not get to escape a God's unwanted attention. Look at what Zeus and Poseidon did to Asteria, your only sister: one sent her racing into the water, the other, it is said, held her prisoner underwater forever. The kindest rumours say she turned into an island plagued by storms and thunder – no, it is better to try to outrun him, even if in the end it is futile. At least try – maybe, just *maybe* you will be the exception.

*How do you stop a Goddess from hunting you, from trying to turn you into an ending?*

Her ire has turned every land against you, you feel her eyes upon you as you struggle out at sea. You turn the ache in your bones from rowing into love and ferocity for your tightening stomach. Yes, what is growing inside you may have been his fault, but you are so tender-hearted you cannot help but love them. A part of you has always known motherhood is your destiny, you are Goddess of it after all. Your children make you stronger, you are sure of it, they make you driven enough to face chthonic, unbeatable creatures, and even the wrath of Goddesses that make every land across the world shun you in your pregnancy. You were Mary long before the world knew Jesus would be born.

*How do you become the mother of the most fearsome Gods?*

You use your gift for seeing what is hidden, you learn to stand over oceans, you shake open the heavens, you follow the signs in a dream to the island that was once your own dear sister, know that nothing mortal or divine can touch you here, she was always your greatest protector. Nine days you spend here in toil, lionesses watch over you, and your sister whispers to her birds to bring you water. You do this for your children, for if there is anyone who can avenge your humiliation, it is them, so you tame the pain within you till it delivers their glory. When they are born you understand why it took all of your body and soul to defend them. After all, it was only your chosen womb that could carry the sun and his sister the moon.

# House of Hyperion, Titan of Light

### 1. Helios, the Sun

'You make my mouth burn for you,' murmurs Apollo to me softly, touching my warm, golden skin. His own shines brightly next to mine. *My light, I am only kindling. Do not fall so deep in love with me.*

He laughs, covers my mouth with his, forgets how I am a burning building and always have been.

He will remember soon. When I cost him a son who he loves more than he could ever love me. We will stop looking each other in the eye one day. Strange what happens to love when it becomes a chore. Something we are forced to do together. Until one day one of you asks to do it alone.

And the next day, and the next day and the day after that.

I warned him I was kindling.

I suppose he didn't taste the burning when we kissed, or maybe he tasted it and didn't think it would burn him, that because the ashes didn't leave my mouth, they were never there at all, but they were. They *were*.

It is like drowning when a God forgets how to love you. It is like they start wildfires, and end in embers of themselves.

2. Selene, the Moon

Everything falls in love under my gaze. The flowers whisper in the wind how they need each other. The ocean softens herself and kisses the cliffs, promising them she will never leave them. Mortals steal away into the night for their first kisses in dark corners, but I find them, bathe them in my light for love. Love is nothing to be ashamed of. It doesn't matter who you love, as long as they fill your heart to the brim with joy, bring you courage where you feel you have none.

I am a romantic, of course. Can you imagine me being anything else? I fell in love with a mortal. Perhaps it was the forbidden nature of it that made us love each other even more. My family's ire when they found out knew no bounds, but I was defiant.

I promised them that I would cease to glow. There would be no more moonlight for their trysts, the seas and oceans would seethe and storm, Nyx would rule now and forever more, and they let me have him.

I should have known. It was a flicker, his life compared to mine. A mortal cannot love a God; they are meant for Hades in the end, and we are to be endless, but I would give up my endless in a heartbeat for him.

Instead, I wrapped him in my shaking arms as he died, asked my niece Artemis for help.

'Take him and turn him into a legacy,' I begged.

She took him and turned him into the majestic creature you call the wolf.

3. Eos, the Dawn

'We cannot do this,' I whisper to Ares as he kisses my rosy fingers, before I use them to open the gates of my father's home in the east.

He laughs and asks me, 'What are you afraid of?'

I bite my lip. *Of everything. But mostly, of crossing the Goddess of Love, who has a cruel sense of humour. And you are hers. Women like her, they never punish their man, they punish the woman who was with him.*

He kisses my worried brow. 'You are too anxious. Come, she has many lovers, she cannot stop me from loving another too.'

*But you are her favourite* ... everything about Ares screams danger but I cannot help it. He knows how to break open something forgotten inside me.

*So what if he is the God of War*, I say to myself as I allow myself to sink into his arms, fissions of pleasure erupting in my veins. The wars he makes aren't for Gods, they are for mortals.

Centuries later, I will lose my son to Troy. In a battlefield scorched in crimson and steel, I will lift his lifeless body and hold him close, tears blurring my vision. *He isn't even a man yet*, I will whisper, smoothing his hairless face with the same fingers I once used to smooth his father's brow.

And somewhere in the skies, I will hear Aphrodite's spiteful laugh as tears streak down my cheeks.

The punishment for stealing in the art of love is unforgivable and perpetual. Ares was wrong.

I should have known. I should have known. *I should have known.*

# Gaia Teaches Rhea Retribution

Mothers are not meant to have a favourite child,
but Rhea was Gaia's favourite. She saw herself
in Rhea, knew what it was like to be underestimated.

They were both quiet nurturers, kind givers.
Yet their own family took their generosity for weakness
and often saw their softness as their disadvantage.

No one believed Gaia or Rhea were capable
of destruction, of vengeance, which is
why even their own husbands took them for granted.

If you practise brutality on a kind woman long enough
you force them to work with their crueler instincts to
survive.
And mothers can become lionesses to keep their cubs
alive.

This is how the Earth found a way to bring
the Sky to his knees, practised patience
and used that time she hoarded as a key,

styled an adamantine scythe, gave it to her own son
Kronos to carve away Ouranos's Godhood.
And when Kronos became power mad and devoured

his own children, she did what any good mother
would do. Taught Rhea the same trick, to teach
her child-devouring husband a lesson.

Over cups of ambrosia, Gaia taught her daughter
guile, trickery, the theft of patience, and how to turn her
own softness, his underestimation, into an instrument.

No one would expect obedient, quiet Rhea
to be the downfall of her husband,
that she would have the wit to manipulate prophecies,

have the cunning to hide her last son Zeus,
then shape him into the blade that would slash
his father's belly, free his siblings, avenge his mother,

remind him that without love for his family,
he is no king or Titan. What they did not know
was they would set into motion a ten thousand

year war between the Gods in their quest
for revenge and retribution. How each would
lose children and grandchildren

in this power struggle they had started.
There is a lesson here,
a lesson about retribution,

they forget that there is always a caveat,
a whispered addendum. Even the heavens
are not exempt from the violence which will visit

if they are disrupt the natural order by ripping a child
from their mother. Even Gods should know better
than to challenge that kind of ancient wisdom,

for there is nothing but ruin in store for deities
and mortals alike when they dare trespass upon
the unconditional love of a mother.

# The Titanomachy

War should have been the pretty thing they promised each other it would be, amid battle cries and songs. The rise of new Gods against old should have been tainted in glory, simply glory.

Instead, Hades glides silently over battlefields so metallic they reflected the twilight glow, and one almost forgot that Gods bled gold. His feet stained with ichor, he tries not to think of the blood as the family he could have known. Ichor turns his black robes gold, giving him a sickening kind of majesty to being the last one standing in an empty war zone. This could have been your uncle's, this could have been your cousin's, this one could have been your friend's.

*Now we will never know.*

Hera cannot stop washing the hem of her dress. It feels like the blood there will never leave. She is holding back her tears, the Queen-to-be of the Heavens is not allowed the mortal act of crying. But she cannot remember who the golden honey-like blood staining her dress belongs to. Was it her father? Was it her aunt? How many of her own met their painful imprisonment at the end of her hands today? She gives up on the hem, lets it lie wetly against her tired, war-worn skin, tosses water on her face to hide her tears, but she can still taste the salt.

*And for the first and only time, she wishes she was mortal enough to allow herself her own tears.*

Gaia feels her children and grandchildren draw blood from each other, their battle waging upon her body. She causes earthquakes to stop them, so instead they wage bloodshed in the sky. She sends her children help in the form of monsters half-hearted, for it is her grandchildren they are going to destroy. She pleads and begs for them to stop but no one heeds her voice; they are too hungry for a power so destructive that it has killed many before them. Gaia is primordial. She is the only one who understands. No matter who wins, she knows she will lose.

*The problem with a mother's love is that it is so unconditional that her grief becomes unconditional too.*

A universe in collapse is both ugly and beautiful. Kronos watches the stars explode before him. Whole planets disintegrated which once held life. Histories of lesser deities wiped away in a heartbeat. All because of his selfishness, his need to control, to fight the prophecy which he had helped create. *Your son will destroy you*, his father had warned, *as you have destroyed me*. All that is left of his legacy is rusted, broken blades and shields in a forgotten bastion that once held never-ending fountains of wine and laughing divinity as far as the eye could see. He catches his exhausted reflection in the mirror and lets out a slow breath, the dust dancing through rays of the sun that drip in from cracks in the walls, in the ceilings.

*This is what the end of a Godhood looks like. A lonely king surveying what was once a kingdom that sang in the clouds now nothing but ash. Waiting for his turn to be cut into pieces, Tartarus calling his name.*

War should have been the prettiest thing dipped in glory. Instead, it is ten thousand years of ichor dripping like rain from the skies, bathing a crying mother in the blood of her own children. Ten thousand years of family bleeding out family, the young making monsters of the old and the old devouring on the new.

# 3. A Mortal Interlude

There is a difference between holy and pure.
Holy is also the way the anger boils inside our throats,
the forgotten in us that carves at our bellies,
the need to turn the heavens themselves inside out
when they twist the knife, and laugh, laugh, laugh.

Unlearn holy as gentle. This is the lie we have all been
feeding each other, mother to daughter, asking the calm
within us to braid our hair, to touch a cool palm to our
cheeks, remind us every night that anger will return ten
fold if we do not control it. Forgive, forgive, forgive.

Pure is what they measure out for us, like we are
their personal recipes. As though we are made for
practice, not for ourselves. A cup of softness, half a bowl
of innocence, a bucket full of virginity, pretend our
prison is our feast while *they* devour, devour, devour.

We know better now. We face fires hand in hand.
We look at each other and say the words each of us
needs to hear. We let the anger boil and let loose flame
by volatile flame. We smile, sacred burning, burning,
burning,
  *and reincarnate.*

*The Olympians*

'From the Gods enthroned
on the awesome rowing-bench
there comes a violent love.'

—Aeschylus, *The Oresteia* (458 BC)

# Young Zeus: The Crossroads

Almost God boy, standing at
the edge of your own abyss,

weighing out your burden to be
the enslaver of your own Titan family,

or to turn it all away, stay hidden
on this gentle Cretan island.

You still doubt the meaning
of your own heritage, don't you?

Still wonder if a God
can change his destiny.

But you do remember
how your father tried to change his.

Instead, he ended up cursed,
and in turn you too, unborn,

became a part of a prophecy.
Tell me, Zeus, if you had a choice,

would you choose true greatness
or being the king of the Gods?

Would you choose love,
or will you need the sin

that comes with the endless power,
the corruption you may succumb to?

Tell me, Zeus, if you had a choice,
what is worthier of your soul?

A throne cast in blood and terror?
Or a life made of happiness but ordinary?

Choose wisely.
History depends upon it.

## Metis and Zeus

*1st Century*

The Titanide who will one day be his first wife knows him well enough to set his bones on ice.

'Between all this Godhood and all this fear,' she chides him, 'you will crush yourself. The weight is too much.'

He sighs, shoulders slumped under the weight of his destiny. 'So take it from me, take it and give it to someone else.'

She smiles, a smile as cunning as a fox about to outsmart its prey, says nothing, but knows all.

*2nd Century*

She is patient with him, even when he does not deserve it. She treats his lack of discipline like it is her virtue to teach him how to do better. Every time he comes close to giving up mastering the ability of thunder, of the weapons, she reminds him, 'Fight for something that is worth dying for – that is the only way to win a war.'

He thinks, and comes up empty-handed over and over again.

Finally, unable to see him crushed any more, she gives it to him.

'I promise, if you win this, you will never feel alone again.'

His smile that day could rival the bluest sky after a fresh wash of rain, his heart thunders in his throat, in his chest. All he can hear is the beating of his own almost-heart in his ears. So loud, he doesn't see the dread in her eyes.

*3rd Century*

'Sometimes you succumb to pettiness and you do not know how to control your rage.' She observes him carefully, watching him curse an entire mountain to crumble at his feet when he cannot climb it.

He hangs his head in shame, he is aware of his hubris, and discomfort is the emotion he handles most poorly.

As he turns to her, about to apologise, he sees she has lifted a corner of her mouth like the crescent blaze of a sickle. 'Good. Now we know we must use that.'

*Aftermath*

Two ivory thrones gleam before them – the only un-
touched, unharmed part of an otherwise dilapidated
palace. A reward for years and years of training, and a
ten thousand-year battle. 'This is yours,' she says warm-
ly, and touches her hand to her womb feeling the shin-
ing life growing in there. 'Ours.'

She is too lost in love, glory and waning bloodlust to see
the colour of his irises as he looks at her. The shade of a
fox's as it looks upon its prey.

# Metis, the Forgotten King Maker

Is there a word for this?
The waiting before the devouring.
The knowing and unknowing
of what is soon to be the ruins of you.

He is a God-King after all.
And I just his consort.
So what if I was his king maker.
Better women than me

have made gentler kings
and still met their ends.
People think having the power of prophecy
and cunning means you can avoid your fate.

No, my loves,
you are simply driven mad
by the knowledge of what is coming
and that you cannot stop it.

Until you learn the way I did,
how to alter a foretelling's truth,
weaponise sadness and deconstruct it
into a life that works for you.

# The Metamorphoses of Zeus
(An Abuser Regrets and Remembers)

How does a boy
who has destroyed his own father
to be crowned a God-King

stop himself
from becoming
a lost and isolated thing?

He destroys.
He devastates.
He devours.

He doesn't ask.
He teaches himself
apologies are for the weak.

After all, the only way
to stop guilt from consuming you
is to consume it first.

Pretend it doesn't exist.
It is the only way to stop it.
This will work ...
            ... it *has* to.

Ghosts in onyx and marble.
Haunted in his dreams.
*Look at what you did.*

*Look at your destruction.*
*Look at all the tatters*
*you have left of everyone*
       *you ever touched.*

# The Making of a God-Queen
(How Hera Survived Trauma)

You were once just a girl who loved birds. You believed it was the nature of your divinity to heal tender winged beings because you thought you were one of them. You cared for each injured one you found. Until trauma made you stop. Until *the tenderness in you hardened.* And this is what you learn from loving something more than yourself in your girlhood:

1. An injured cuckoo is sometimes a lascivious God in disguise waiting for you to cradle him so he can turn and ravage your youth.
2. Small, hopeful things often lead painfully short lives and you are too immortal to become one of them.
3. Adapt. Regain composure. Do not let him have the upper hand. Before he finds a way to shame you. Marry him and become the bridge he could never burn, never forget. No matter how much he tries to.

And *this* is what you learn from nurturing snakes instead of birds:

1. Soon they become your dearest friends.
2. You grow immune to every kind of poison.

And *this* is what becomes of you when he betrays your bed for another's night after night:

1. Your grief twists inside your gut till it becomes venomous breath.
2. You grit your teeth and smile fork-tongued through the tragedy.

And *this* is what happens when he denies you your wishes and you do not know how to punish him in any other way.

1. You poison every other woman he ever touches.
2. You demolish all his children with them.
3. You make him bleed.
        You make him bleed.
            *You make him bleed …*

# Hymn for Hera

She finds it difficult to cry.
Rage suppresses her tears.
She has shed her girlhood,
traded her emotions for power.

It is easier to be hated
than to face not being loved.
Easier to be angry
than accept sadness.

But we all have to let
the sorrow out somehow.
So she takes the souls
of the clouds and ties

them to her own.
Every time Zeus
and she fight, the clouds,
like her heartache, overflow.

Zeus may have been the God
of lightning and of thunder.

But it was Hera
who invented the rain.

# Hera, After

*How do you explain leaving*
*to someone who was never there at all?*

Years later, they will ask her what drove her to finally do
it. And she will say it was the empty house, or the loneli-
ness that had wedged itself so firmly between them, or
how cold the onyx floors of Olympus felt without the
bare feet of Gods constantly walking over them.

She will lie, of course. For all her changes, she still
believed she was Goddess enough not to owe anyone
the truth about her life.

Still, the truth does exist. It lies sitting inside a drawer at
her mahogany desk, and whenever a storm brews

outside she remembers.

Inside the drawer is a thunderbolt. Ancient. Fatal.
Sheathed in an azure box crafted by Hephaestus for her
jewellery once, now filled with a thundercloud to keep
the electric nature of this element alive. She is unafraid
as she lifts it out of the box and holds it like a harmless
little toy, although once, she used to be terrified of it.
Her husband had convinced everyone that he was the
only one capable and powerful enough to control these,
and for millennia she believed him. They all did. Now,
wiser and more evolved to the reasons why lies are told

and how much he lied, and with this in her possession, she pictures his face when she would not tolerate the way he treated her and their marriage any more.

She remembers that day. Zeus, drunk, the other Gods and Goddesses all gone, lost in his loneliness, deluded by his own grandeur, staggering, as she watched him in disgust. His pride and his pathological need for the unquestioning devotion from everyone around him made him incapable of understanding that their children, their family chose to adapt to the new millennia and leave. She had tried explaining this to him, even through her own grief. Children leave. People leave. It is what they do. Enjoy them while they are with you, but do not fall apart when they are not. He, however, would not listen. Forever bull-headed about his convictions, it had led him to drink till he no longer even remotely resembled the all-powerful Sky-God he once was.

Around her, the implications of this were visible in the once unbreakable marble. He had begun using the pillars of their home for target practice, had forgotten that without the other Gods and their powers, Olympus became closer to mortal buildings that crumble and fall than to its mighty immortality.

Or maybe he remembered. And he just didn't care.

Both seemed equally likely.

When he reached for this thunderbolt, she took his arm to stop him.

But his impulses were what made him, and he had never been one to be stopped from anything he desired.

So he did the unforgivable. His mighty arm flung her off him, tossing her across the corridor into a pillar that then proceeded to fall apart.

For a second, all was still. And then, as her eyes looked upon him, narrowed, blazing, the tremors began to hit. The first one knocked him off his feet. The second took the already crumbling pillars, the third every inch of the onyx floors, cracked and broke and fell apart until there was nothing left, other than her.

It took her a few moments to realise that her right hand had managed to take the thunderbolt he had meant to reach for. Gods do not divorce, and by a cruel twist of fate, she was the Goddess of marriage too.

So, instead, she took this, his last thunderbolt and left him there, somewhere in the rubble. She took nothing with her, just her dignity and a heart that needed to atone.

Somewhere in the destruction of her home, she had found the truth. She had been punishing victim after victim of her husband when she should have been looking to free them all and herself too.

When you are immortal, she supposed, there was always time to atone.

And now, sitting at her desk, she silently puts the thunderbolt back in its box just as her door opens. 'Miss Hera?' asks a little voice. 'They've brought the new girls here to meet you.'

Hera smiles at the young woman at the door. 'Thank you, Io.'

As she rises from her chair and walks out the door, she takes a second to straighten the sign on the front. The one that reads:

> *Hera O.*
> *Director and Founder*
> *The Sisterhood to Aid Women Suffering Abuse.*

Who says change is an impossible thing
after a certain age, when all of life
is nothing but the act of changing to grow?

# Zeus, After

*'I hope you are loved in the way you deserve.'*
*Depending on who you are, and what you have done,*
*those words could be the kindest wish or the worst curse.*

He didn't know what people expected of him. Back in the day, he could do anything he wanted and no one and nothing could hold him back. He was a *God-King*! Didn't these small, ridiculous mortals understand?

No, of course they didn't. He paced his office then paused and looked down. Forty storeys up, everything down there looked like an ant colony. It wasn't Olympus, but it was as close as he could get to it, and he wasn't ready to let go just because some women had complained he was a rapist. *Rapist*, what did that word even mean? They should all feel fortunate, they got a chance to be in the presence of a God.

His fists clenched when he involuntarily remembered what his wife had once half threatened, half warned him. *'There will come a day when you will be powerless and will be held accountable. You are too reckless to be loved but you crave love all the same.'*

But Gods are never powerless, or so he believed. Now he knew better; Gods are never powerless, not until they are stripped of those who believe and worship them.

After millennia of power, this is what had happened to them. The rest had chosen to leave and to adapt. He had been the last to do so. When his wife had finally disappeared, leaving their home in rubble, he had been forced to leave too.

*'You will learn the meaning of regret well.'*

His charms had aided him, of course. Anyone who could smoothly talk their way into anything and commanded a presence was welcome in this strange culture of 'economy rules all' that mortals had created. He had flourished and risen through the business world.

Things on earth had changed. Women were ... different. People actually called the seduction women did not want a different word and to act on that impulse was a crime.

It didn't stop him, though. It never had. He had learned quickly how to silence them, how to do what he saw other powerful people do, buy his way out through muscle, through blackmail, through ultimate betrayal.

*'It will be someone you believe to be weak and defenseless who will bring you to your knees.'*

His comeuppance came in the form of a small, quiet girl at a bar. Something about her spoke fire to him. She said no, once, twice, a hundred times. It did not stop him. But this one, she would not go away. Everything he threw at her, she fought back – no blackmail, no threats, no non-disclosure agreements worked. She took to the internet and told her story over and over again till the world heard. And then the others began to come out of the shadows.

Every woman he had ever wronged.

*'Even God-Kings have to answer for their sins.'*

'Sir.' A knock on his door from his secretary. 'Sir, the police are here and they want to speak to you. I don't think I can hold them back much longer. They have a warrant.'

*'You will be at the mercy of the same beings you once made human from clay.'*

When he did not answer, the knocking grew more incessant and he could hear more voices, murmuring, loud. Though they are muffled, he knows what they are saying.

His head dropped for a second and he tried to think of someone to pray to. Coming up hollow, he sighed, in frustration. Then composed himself, straightened his suit, pulled himself up to his height.

*'When it happens, I hope you face your downfall with the dignity of a king.'*

She was right. She had always been right. At last, he took a deep breath and cleared his throat.

'Let them in.'

## Athena Rises

Her heart wears wisdom skin
and wit-warmed splendour,
the echoes of a war cry holding
its four chambers together.

A manifestation of wisdom
and her mother's ambitions,
grey eyes like flashing steel
bringing her father to contrition.

She rises over Olympus
on a night of victory dancing,
she rises like the blood moon
in a sky of a thousand stars bursting.

# A Place to Find Purpose

To craft purpose from birth is no easy task.
Not even if you are Goddess destined
and Olympus given. Not when
you are eyed with suspicion

and every God has a bet
to catch you mid misstep,
because it unnerves them
how you are both wisdom and woman.

The problem, of course,
is being too unusual and too clever.
It draws Hera's ire and Zeus's favour.
You prefer books to people.

You are quiet. Always in contemplation,
more powerful in your solitude, but where
do you find silence on this mountain
brimming with gossiping, raucous immortals?

That's why you did it, didn't you, Athena?
When you couldn't find a place of solitude,
you built it, the first ever library –
the library of Alexandria.

# Athena's Tale

*Razor-sharp lips rise*
*in a twisted little smile.*
*'Go on.' Her hand tightens*
*on her sword. 'Challenge me.'*

The insides of a God are very different from the insides of a man. Where man has a heart, lungs, other organs that facilitate his existence, the insides of a God are no different from the insides of a universe. Gleaming stars conspire. Galaxies burst and die. No one sees any of this happen, however. Not unless you have been devoured by a God, doomed to float across this pseudo-universe forever.

Her birth, her true birth was lonely. As her cries filled up the darkness and comets escaped, her mother busily swaddled her in a blanket she had stitched from stardust. Her mother's arms are strong, capable and absolutely no-nonsense.

She is a babe for the span of minutes and then her limbs grow longer, as this is the way of all the Gods: no one gets to stay a child for long. Metis's recovery is quick too, immortality and her Titanide blood ensure that. This is also why she did not die when Zeus swallowed her, although she is still unsure if that was a kindness or ... Not one to waste any time, Metis takes her daughter's chin. 'Listen to me, girl.'

The girl, startled, new to existence and still wide-eyed can just about manage a nod.

'When you leave here, you are going to be the wisest and the most powerful of all the Gods. Your name is Athena. And you will make sure they remember you the way they will choose not to remember me. Understand?'

*If you guard yourself well, no one will ever do to you what was done to me.*

The girl's flashing eyes may be new to the world. But she understands the gravity of this sort of promise well. Something intrinsic inside us all does, when we make a contract like this with our parents. Her eyes harden in that second, agate stones that look too old for her face. 'Yes, Mother.'

There is a reason why the word 'meticulous' comes from her mother's name. Metis has, in the course of her pregnancy, carefully turned Zeus's insides into a map.

Here was where the precious metals could be mined, this was where she could find spools of stardust to turn into robes. She turns the blood of planets into cloth; there is no end to what the Titanide can do. All the while Athena follows, watches, learns. This is all part of her education. Her mother shows her how to make the best of terrible situations, how to customise wisdom into a weapon.

She is less mother, more teacher. Revenge has consumed every part of her that once held deep, soft love. Zeus hadn't just devoured her, he had also demolished every single part of her that once knew how to love anything. All that was left for Athena was Metis's skills as a teacher, and like her agate stone eyes, the child in her began to develop sharper edges.

'Do not,' warns Metis as she watches her daughter develop the fine, pointed look of a spear, 'fall prey to hubris. It will be the downfall of your father and it will be the downfall of your legacy too if you are not careful.'

Athena nods. She doesn't yet know it is the only promise she will not keep to her mother.

*Hubris is a lethal infection and it brings us dangerously close to mortals when we fall prey to it.*

Athena is born with a war cry on her lips, and her mother's promise in her heart. Fully clothed in robes made from the blood of planets, a helmet and a shield of steel that comes from the hearts of stars themselves, she looks like the blood moon at solstice. So astonishing is her birth that Zeus forgets his head had to be split wide open for it. She is his favourite before she even opens her mouth. He spins a tale about how she is motherless. How she is his daughter alone, how he alone created her.

She is wise enough to know how to say nothing when he does this.

She sees a flash of her mother in her father's eyes sometimes. A warning.

*Of all the Gods, your father is the one you must trust least, but remember to always be his favourite.*

She falls in love with architecture, her fascination around the building and sustaining of these metropolises. Cities by the sea are her favourite to collect. Her mind is full of secrets and she needs to occupy herself, after all.

One of her many secrets is that she is the only God who knows that time is not linear. It is an illusion Kronos has put on the universe to punish them all for rejecting him. Her mother shows her how to see through it. Those who have the gift of prophecy – Apollo, Prometheus – simply know how to pierce through the illusion. Athena does too. She just keeps it to herself.

*If you push at the veil it falls apart. Knowledge is power, knowledge is everything.*

Poseidon grows envious. She is encroaching on his territories. She ignores him.

It is dangerous to challenge an old God this way, but the metal to her spear is as sharp as her mind, and she is unafraid of him.

*Your name is Athena, daughter of Metis. Never forget that.*

They spar, the way Gods spar, with a mortal audience to cheer and clap the miraculous things they can do. Poseidon creates the bluest of saltwater springs, soft and serene to add to the mystique of the city, but does little else except add a bit of beauty. But Athena, who understood the way cities survive, knows how to facilitate its economy. She rests on her knees and plants a single seed into the soft earth. An eruption, a breaking, the earth shudders, and from seedling sprouts the sprig and then the trunk of a fast-growing olive tree. The fruit was vast and bountiful, and it was the only one which could live long and well in an arid land. The oil from the olives can be used to warm the houses that are chilled by the winds of the sea by night.

Practicality, another gift from her mother.

They name the city Athens after her. Poseidon is enraged, and the sea blackens and stirs into the most chaotic of all his storms. He threatens to destroy the city, and tells Athena there is restitution to be paid for dishonouring an older God this way.

Athena bears him no mind.

She has never been afraid of anyone. Not when she is already at checkmate when they have just moved the first pawn. This is what her mother has taught her.

But the umbrages of old Gods against the new are as timeless as Chaos herself.

Her only mistake. And her costliest one.

Poseidon *will* choose another time, another day, another way to dishonour her in return. She is just too proud to think him harmful … yet. Too taken in by her own victory. Too quick to underestimate those who do not match her wits.

*Be careful of hubris. For it is the undoing of all the Gods.*

# Athena, After

The old Gods
may be ash and bone now,
but in us they rise anew.

Did you think Athena would just disappear
when there are so many little girls
she has yet to help become warriors too?

She, the marrow of invention,
a story wrapped in the ribcage
of every hero who has mastered the art of war.

She, who rewards wisdom and bravery;
when my daughter asks how to fight monsters
Athena is who I will tell her to look for.

I will take her to the library,
and introduce her to every librarian
because they are where Athena lives now.

# Pallas and Athena

They named her 'virgin'
for they could not handle her autonomy
in her carnality, her preference.

She shunned Gods and men alike,
so they rumoured her chaste,
but perhaps their dismissal was in haste.

Her desires lay elsewhere, you see.
A girl just like her, but born of the sea.
Fire in her eyes, a mouth made for war cries,

long silver hair like her merman father,
both of then raised under his mild but firm hand,
for Triton was a better parent than Zeus even as a foster.

Their days filled with rituals of steel and sacrifice
melted away into nights filled with worship,
holding each other like a prayer unspoken;

this was floating in the cloud,
this was every flavour of a star bursting,
two girlhoods linking into a womanhood unbroken.

But fate does not allow an immortal
the luxury to love a mortal forever,
not even if they promise it to each other.

A friendly spar before the Gods that should
have ended in two accomplished warriors
being blessed by the divinity that was watching,

ends instead in a diversion, a mistake, an impaling. Rivers
of crimson on an aegis, turning the marble
it touches holy, a lover holding the body of a lover,

cursing providence and promising
if she could not have her,
then there would never be another.

If you want to know the sinews
of the eternity in a love
crafted woman to woman,

ask Athena why she never loved again,
and why she carries that sobriquet ahead
of her own name, first Pallas, then Athena.

## The Birth of Ares

What else could have come
from a love that became so brutal
even the skies pelted hailstones
and hurricanes when they fought?

Confrontation. Combat. Combustion.
Still the son of two of the mightiest Gods.
But a child born of such rage
will always smell of sulphur and damage.

The God he becomes stands on
warcries and bones and death
in a battlefield. Who else could he be
with the eternal screaming in his head?

# War and Poetry

Ares, of warfare, soldiers, tributes,
Ares, of carnage, widow-making
and eternal cries, the sickening sound
of a sword sinking to flesh,

Ares, God of terrible things.
Ares, of screams, of screams,
                    *of screams.*

It is the mothers' prayers that sent her
to him. They prayed for clemency, mercy
to any softer God listening and it is
Calliope who heard their inconsolable pain.

This compassionate Goddess of poetry,
oldest of the Muse sisters ascended Olympus
to reason with the God of War,
even to spar with him if need be.

Instead, she found him, clutching his head,
unable to stand the carnage within him,
teeth clenched, close to screaming.
She asked him why, why he couldn't stop,

and he lifted his head, eyes red, and said,
'No one taught me how to stop the bloodshed,
the clash of metal, the battle cries,
and all the tragedy and the screaming.'

So Calliope tenderly took his hands
away from his head, and whispered to him
a soothing story in verse. Calliope, alone
who he listened to, who helped him fell

each demon in his head and brought
peace to the God of War and the earth.
To this day if a conflict ceases, it is thanks
to the kindness of Calliope, Goddess of Epic Poetry,

bringer of peace, infusing kindness gently
steeped with poetry to soothe a tired War God's head.

# Ares, After

*Sometimes I pray for the living in me,*
*And sometimes I pray for the dead.*

His father refused to tell him any stories, and his mother would never sing him any lullabies. They were both negligent. Perhaps this is why he turned out the way he did.

At least, that's what his therapist thought.

He should have been at his happiest, really. Humans never stop going to war and his name is forever etched in their blood. Battlefield after battlefield donates souls to his cause. Countries continue to fight over manmade borders. Some name each other foe and then friend, then the foes are friends and the friends foes.

And they have the audacity to call the Gods fickle.

But Ares knows the truth now, the force that drives this. War makes the very wealthy richer so they engineer thousands of them.

*It should have pleased him to still have tributes when the others have none.*

Instead, he was tired. All the time. What he was God of was against his own nature. He didn't want to be the reason why young men lost their lives because old men said they had to. He didn't want greed to win. The non-stop screaming, the clang of metal against metal was going to kill him, he was sure of it.

It was what he prayed for every night.

He spent longer in bed that he needed to these days. Lost job after job because all he knew was chaos and this mortal world was obsessed with order. He was ordered by the court to go to a therapist because of the last bar fight he was in. If there was something he still knew how to do, it was brawl.

The only job he could keep was illegal boxing, where there were no rules. Well, there were two rules. Rule 1: Leave the other man worse off, and Rule 2: Try to get out alive. It paid well and he never lost. He tried not to think about the crimson blood on his knuckles being the last time a man was seen alive.

It's how he kept his apartment. Bottles littered the floor. His therapist gave him Prozac for intermittent explosive disorder. He didn't know that it takes more than a whole bottle at once to sedate a God. Ichor doesn't take kindly to antidepressants.

He is lonely beyond lonely. Every organ in him cries out for someone who knows him for who he was without demanding he make use of his terrible powers. *Who will want you like this*, he thinks disgustedly as he stares at his tired face in the mirror. *Everyone who has ever loved you has never been able to tolerate your company. They called you a stupid brute on Olympus, made you feel unworthy of being Zeus's son for good reason.*

He has never been more powerful than any of the others and he has never felt more lost.

His powers are suitable for a general at war. On this human plane, in this bustling city, he feels like another face in the crowd.

Sometimes Aphrodite visits him.

She is still beautiful and she is thriving. All these New Age tools have only made her stronger. There are eight billion mortals looking for a real love to keep her powerful. Aphrodite knows how to adapt the way water does. It makes sense. After all, she was born of the sea.

Once, when she visits, she asks him, 'Why are you so unhappy? You could have it all, a job in military intelligence, a mansion, a thousand women.' She has not been jealous since she discovered Hephaestus is the only one who will ever hold her heart. What she doesn't tell him: *'You don't have to live like this.'*

*Do you think War-Gods ever long for contentment? Do you think peace ever makes its way into their souls?*

He wants to reach for her because she is the only shining being who cares. But that would be the loneliness talking again. 'I want none of it.' He doesn't say, *'I want someone who stays.'*

'What do you want?' she asks him, gently.

'I want what you and Hephaestus have,' he says to her. 'A love of equals that knows all of me, but doesn't judge me for my regrets. A love that knows I would never ever judge them and love them completely.'

Aphrodite smiles like the enigma she is. 'Why didn't you say so before?'

She's gone before he can ask what she is talking about.

Days later, he is sitting in a club, drinking after a fight. He's sat at this same place for centuries now. Things have changed, people have changed, the owners have changed.

But there is still a comfort here, a familiarity he clings to. It's open mic night and poet after musician takes the stage. He isn't listening, his head addled in whisky.

He hears her before he sees her.

Eloquence personified, Homeric in her hymn, she weaves the tale of the God of War and a Muse who once loved each other. How somewhere in the sands of time through all this change, they lost each other. When she brings her tale to a close, the audience breaks out of the spell and so does he.

Heart pounding, he raises his glass in her direction, and she makes her way through the audience to him.

'It's been a long time, Ares.'

He inhales sharply as she reaches over and hugs him, stiffening but then melting into her arms. It felt like a burden as heavy as what Atlas carried was slipping from his shoulders… He raises his bruised knuckles to touch her face. "It is good to see you, Calliope. Would you like to join me for a drink?'

Her hand gently settling on his as it touched her skin. She looks at her watch and smiles. 'Why not? We only have forever.'

# Craving (A synonym for Aphrodite)

Who can say craving without
letting their tongue dance past
the lust within the vowels.

A stirring, something primal,
one of the few things we have
left in common with animals.

Perhaps it makes sense then,
the story of her birth sounds
so vulgar. How the sea waves

that became her mother
mixed with the still-bloodied
parts that were once her father.

Danger. Everything about her
spelled the kind of danger
that could make order crumble.

Of course, they would try to crush
what they couldn't understand.
Not when the hunger in her alone

could swallow up every God,
every woman, every man,
every person, the whole universe.

# The Goddess of Love: Aphrodite

She is supposed to be love.
The perfection of it.
The embodiment of it.
The splendour of it.

Mortals and Gods alike
look at her and think,
how marvellous it must be
to be the Goddess of Love.

Aphrodite, the Goddess
of breathless romances,
of honeyed breaths,
of feverishly promised forevers.

They are too blind to see
how often love is smoke
and mirrors, used to ensnare
like a hunter does a stag.

Aphrodite, the Goddess
of unrequited ruins,
of lifetimes of unhappiness,
of forgotten fallen kingdoms.

What good is it to be the Goddess
of Love when you cannot be
the Goddess of Kindness,
of pure intentions too?

## Love and War

*Who else was it going to be*
*other than him when I am me?*

We are both destruction and evolution,
endings and beginnings.

The universe plots to bring
those who can heal each other together.

Yet I do not call this healing.
This is something else.

A challenge. Unpredictable. With the others,
it is easier to keep pieces of myself.

Hermes got my humour and hubris,
Adonis my purity and passion.

Ares took all of me and made my heart sore.
Because it is untrue what they say.

*Nothing is fair in love or war.*

## Aphrodite's Gift

Of course, it was Prometheus who shaped us
from the most resilient of clay, and Athena
who made our lungs glow with life.

But while the Gods drank in celebration
their minds were too preoccupied
with the tributes they had not yet received

to notice that one of them was missing,
that one of them had disappeared to where
Prometheus lived, a place made of river and wood.

There in a moonlight-steeped workshop, she lifted
each clay figurine with a cryptic smile on her lips,
a red glow emerging from her hands as she did.

Prometheus may be the father to us all,
and Athena our giver of life. But Aphrodite
is responsible for the gift that wrecks us all:

our fragile, hard-loving, hard-falling,
dangerous-to-grip and difficult-to-lose,
spellbinding but treacherous hearts.

# Night Songs to Aphrodite

'Aphrodite,' I pleaded to the moon-
drenched night sky.

'Tell me, if love is meant to heal,
then why does it destroy those who choose it?'

From somewhere beyond the clouds,
I heard the Goddess laugh.

And I knew.

# Aphrodite, After

*Passion is lovely, lilting and limited.*
*Love requires more elegant effort*
*and whole eras dedicated to it.*
*She is a dichotomy,*
*the Goddess of both.*

Elegant. That's the way they describe her. Always in cream suits that complement her dark skin, long hair tied back gracefully in a bun, one would almost miss the magnetic nature of her eyes. But no one could ignore the primal pull in their stomachs when she walked into a room.

For her part, she takes it as a sign of reverence, a new form of tribute. She is the owner of one of the most forward-thinking dating companies after all.

Aphrodite is nothing if not good at adapting. Love has always been about adaptation and evolution. It is hate that never changes. Even the Gods know how to change, how to leave when home becomes a place you cannot remember happiness any more.

They had all been lost when they departed Olympus. Eros had fallen into despair as the ambrosia that kept Psyche alive had lost its power. She died as she was born. Earth bound.

He had spent ten years walking the world a hermit. His arrows lay forgotten in the dust of the Sahara somewhere. When she had finally found him, he was a shadow of the God he had left behind.

Her beautiful boy was despondent, sitting in a dark, dingy alley when she found him. 'No one knows how to love here,' he rasped, and she felt the crushing weight of his sheer disappointment. 'Everything is artificial in this broken realm.'

She touched his forehead, caked with dirt, with sand, with grease. 'Of course they don't know how to love. That is why we still exist. For it is our job to show them.'

Somewhere, a man and the only man he has ever truly loved are celebrating fifty years together. Somewhere else, a girl falls in love with her best friend and finally kisses her. It still feels like the whole world goes silent when two people tell each other they love each other for the first time, even when it does not think those people should be together.

Love can never die, not completely. There were too many romantics, too many *poets*, too many places where lovers could meet and kisses could be shared.

There is still love to be found here. It just needs some-one to whisper it back to life. This is spell work. It is time-consuming, full of errors . . .

. . . but it is not impossible.

They play mortals at their own games. It's Hephaestus's idea. Mortals are the Gods' novelties who are, in turn, always enraptured by novelties; an easy way to manipu-late them is to hold what they are looking for just out of reach.

Perfection in imperfection. Someone whose flaws work well with yours. Infuse modern love with the hues of older romance. An agency that offers something real in a world that was increasingly becoming plastic. Aphro-dite puts her powers into information superhighways with the help of nymphs who have adapted to learn code. Brontes the Cyclops helps Eros to convert his ar-rows into algorithms.

All of this is built on such a whim, it is a wonder that it works.

Slowly, she watches the soft blue of love rise in mortal after mortal. Eros never misses.

It feels like she has finally found her peace. The cruelty in her has turned to kindness. Hephaestus's gentle love has seen to that. And yet ...

Something she cannot name inside her still feels missing.

Hestia contacts her out of the blue. Something about a meeting that she thinks Aphrodite will find beneficial. Hearing from her after so long startles Aphrodite into accepting before realising what she has done.

'I promise,' Hestia tells her, something in her voice like the breeze that carries a wildfire, 'you will love it.'

Aphrodite isn't much different from the family she came from in her curiosity and fascination for novelties.

This ... this was not what she was expecting. She is standing in the doorway of Hestia's cosy cottage. It is filled to the brim with women who are in full conversational sway. Each one is a reformation of sorts in her trade. One thing is for sure, between the warmth of the wooden and soft-hued room and the laughter resonating, Hestia still knew how to put together the most wonderful of gatherings. Each person seemed perfectly chosen to bring out the fire in the people they were talking to.

And for the first time in her life, Aphrodite feels out of place.

Men have always been easy for her. Women … she had spent too much time trying to protect her men from them, she didn't know how to be around them without suspicion, or doubt.

Hestia appears behind her, hands her a glass of wine and gently nudges her forward.

'Stop being silly, and come and join the conversation.'

Aphrodite opens her mouth to protest, to turn back, to run, then closes it again. Finally, she goes against her nature, perches on a comfortable red sofa and lifts the crystal-clear glass to her mouth, a sip of rich wine putting her slightly more at ease.

The women around her add fullness by smiling, laughing, conversing like she has never heard before. There's a comfort here, an easiness she begins to realise she was missing all along.

*Even ancient beings have something new to learn once in a while.*

In all her tens of thousands of years alive she had gone without this kind of friendly, warm company. The company of other women.

# The Blacksmith God

*You should have been King.*
But the Gods are shallow;

instead, the arms that were
meant to love you unconditionally

threw you off a holy mountain
to a wounded, savage fate below.

But was it savage? Away from the cruel
sight of feckless, venomous Gods,

you grew to be kind and unspoiled, sweet Hephaestus.
You learned to turn metal into magic,

made the mortal children toys and helmets
in your adopted village of mortals,

and when you were summoned to Olympus
how the children wept for their gentle friend Hephaestus.

When Zeus tried to give you
the Goddess of Love as an apology –

as if abandonment is easily bandaged
and not a lifelong debt you will forever carry –

you shook your head vehemently.
'Please. No. Do not punish her, or me.'

You knew she loved your brother Ares.
Zeus fixed you with his icy gaze.

'I do not take my word back, boy.'
'But she will never stay with me.'

Hera looks to Zeus, and then to the son
she had forsaken for the first time with sympathy.

'It gets easier. Slowly you too
will learn how to cope with it.'

# Lessons from Hephaestus

*If hate is what made you,*
*how does one replace it with love?*

You learn sweetness despite
being built of jealous commands.

You choose a different path
than your blood demands.

When no one aids you,
you build your own legs.

You learn how to be needed
instead of the easiness of wanted.

And when the burning
inside your chest claws,

insults you as forgotten, hideous,
unloved every single night,

you learn how to create iron, then a sword,
and challenge those demons to a fight.

# The Marriage Bed

Homer, Hesiod, Pindar,
they will tell you that
she was disgusted by him,

that she stole away from
their marriage bed for she saw
nothing but golden shackles.

That Ares held her heart forever
as the man who she shared
too much with as her lover.

But by Olympus, that man,
with his work-worn hands
and his forgiving, steadfast love.

That blacksmith who wore his God-skin
so uneasily, but his heart on his sleeve,
always so much more mortal than the rest.

Sometimes, the poets get it wrong.
We think beauty is for beauty
and passion alone for love.

I suppose a tragic romance
fraught with unhappiness
makes for a better poem

than a love that takes millennia
to grow. But is it so very wrong
to believe the one they called the ugliest

had the loveliest heart, and hearts like his
are far more fertile ground than bloody
battlefields for love, true love, to grow?

# Hephaestus's Tale

*What do you do when you see a love so pure, so completely unwavering other than bow to it?*

*

*They say she was as beautiful as he was hideous. That there was no love lost there. They were wrong.*

On their wedding day, she sobs, and her anguish can be heard outside her dressing chamber. 'I don't want to marry him,' she tells Ares, who is holding her close in his defeated arms. 'Can't you tell your father I don't want to marry him?'

Ares's face is lost between rage and sorrow. 'I've asked. You know what he said.'

Zeus would have his way about this. There were only so many times he would entertain the grievances of other Gods after he had made his decision. Go too far, and you end up working years of labour in Tartarus. And he was hardest on his own sons.

'But not him, Ares.' She doesn't need to say, *'I will never love him like I love you.'*

It's true. She never does.

Hephaestus knows where his wife goes on the nights he does not come back from the volcano. He hears the whispers from the tongues of crueller Gods when he walks past the eastern pillars to his room in the morning. They pretend to be there to watch Helios's ascent. Instead, they gossip about his brother and his wife. 'Poor Hephaestus,' they whisper loudly in mock sympathy, within earshot. 'He has no idea.'

He does. But he cannot find it in his heart to fault her for continuing to love his brother when it is he who has been made her husband by force.

He is patient and he has a gentle heart. His fall from Olympus taught him to have more faith in that it taught him to listen to unkind words designed to hurt.

*They said he was as hideous as she was beautiful. That there was no love lost there.*

He wore his kindness better than he wore his Godhood and never once raised his voice at her. Somewhere along the way, she started to notice the soft things about him. Like how he was always there when she was sad. Silent and waiting.

*They were wrong.*

The first time she visited him within the volcano, the three Cyclopes, Brontes in particular, fussed over her so much she wondered why she had not visited before. They brought her nectar, piled jewellery at her feet, asked over and over again if they should lower the temperature of the dark, molten interiors for her. This was less for her, and more because they wanted a chance to show off how they could make magma cool with a single word, but she does not mind.

She was not sure why she had come down to visit him this time. So many Gods and Goddesses vied for her attentions at this very moment, yet all she could think of was her husband. Which confounded her.

He had never mattered enough before.

It was in the forge that she felt like she was looking at him for the first time. Brontes, the gentlest but also loudest of all the Cyclopes, was proudly leading her to Hephaestus to present her, but she stopped him by gently touching his arm and shaking her head. She wanted to stay hidden, in the shadows, watching him work. He nodded, slightly sulky at the idea he didn't get to watch Hephaestus's expression when he saw Aphrodite, but did as he was told.

Close to a crimson and orange glowing igneous arch-
way she watched as he worked in a way she had never
seen any God on Olympus work. Everything he crafted
was a labour of such careful love. No wonder he came
home with blackened hands, his titanium, prosthetic
leg sometimes smeared with cooling lava.

After a few minutes, it was as though he sensed her; he
lowered his hammer and looked to her.

A smile dawned on her lips.

'It was you, wasn't it? It was always you. Why didn't you
tell me?'

His smile was both rueful and soft all at once. 'You nev-
er asked.'

It was hard to believe that he was Hera's son.

But then he had been cared for by the old mortal man
who found him as a crying, hurt babe at the base of
a mountain, raised in a small village, and his nurture
spoke louder than his genealogy did. He didn't know
any other way than to work for what he had.

His mortal father told him: 'Adapt.'

It was all he knew how to do well.

Strangely, it is the one quality he shared with his wife.

He had seen the cruel side of Aphrodite and the soft side of her, but he had never seen her like this. With all her attention in rapture of him, standing in the forge of all places. When she came to him, he took her hand and she doesn't flinch. Instead, she kisses him as though they have both been drowning all this time and this kiss is the only survival they have.

This was the day he finally understood why she is called the Goddess of Love.

Eros was born not long after this day.

As the baby's wails filled Olympus, the whispers started anew. They thought he was Ares' son, but one look at the boy's molten eyes and gentle disposition told the truth.

Once, over too much heady ambrosia, Hermes asked him how he had made her fall in love. Hephaestus answered, 'When I held her, I held her gently so that she always knew she could fly away and I would never harm her or clip her wings.' When he looked at his wife, his eyes were soft. 'She chose never to leave.'

*They say she was as beautiful as he was hideous. That there was no love lost there.*

*They were wrong.*

# The Sun God

Who else could tame the sun
other than a boy of gold
born melody-souled
and prophecy-tongued.

Poetry in those veins,
healing in his eyes,
but if he so desired
he could turn cities hollow.

The story goes that Midas
had a golden touch, but
if gold could name itself,
it would choose to be named Apollo.

## Apollo's Secret

He found it easier to be friends with women.
His sister Artemis. Athena. The Muses.

Women wanted to know him for more than his power
and his fearsome nature of burning; they spoke about

poetry, archery, healing, music, warmth.
All this he found with women, but men,

he was both in love and hate with them. You see,
when you live forever, people scrutinise you.

You cannot want what you want, or even what you need.
You are expected to fill the world with Gods and Demi-
gods like you.

(So what if all the children are damned and broken.
As if it isn't the legacy of their family to leave broken
children.)

But men made his whole body erupt with passion,
a thousand gleaming suns scorched in his celestial body.

He saw so much of the future at once
he had to invent his Oracles to cope.

He had to do something with all those foresights
that seared his skin, which no one wanted to hear.

So he tried to give away his prophetic powers
to vessel after vessel but never could get rid of the
prophecies.

He tried to be with the mothers to his children
but destroyed them in the all-consuming of himself.

And one day, Aphrodite, who was unable to see
their torment or his, asked him, 'Why, why are you like
this?'

'Because,' he whispered helplessly, almost to himself,
'I don't know how to survive my immortality being any-
thing else.'

If you ever want to know what happens when a God
suppresses a part of himself, look no further than the
trail of ashes behind Apollo.

# Apollo to Icarus

Seeing you come to me should be catharsis
but instead it takes on the colour of murder.

It is because you are the mortal one between us.
More beautiful in your emotion, easier to kill,

all that energy inside you as quickly perishable
as the entire lifespan of a butterfly.

Maybe this was why I wanted you.
I had grown cold with the responsibility for the sun.

Destruction was not what I intended for you,
but this is what happens to all who follow in my wake.

Ask the sunflower who she used to be; she will tell you
she was once a nymph who fell in love with me.

This is the difference between ichor and iron.
The universe made you closer to itself than us.

The water will take better care of you than me.
Let me melt your wings, you belong to the sea.

Now a stillness neither of us knew before.
Now a softness no one can answer for.

# The Moon Goddess

There is something moon-soaked
and dawn-flavoured about her.
Something kissed by the wild
and loved by lightning.

She, the Goddess of storm hunting
and wolves and moonlight magic.
She, the queen of the forest,
of womanhood more brutal than tragic.

# The Moon Writes a Love Letter to Artemis

I choose you, the rarest of beings,
for the belonging I never had with
your aunt Selene. She was meant to be
my mother, my food giver, but I found her
too little in love with me, and more in love
with watching love. But you, dear Artemis,
you with the wings that you made from
your own silver-tipped wishes, how you
always just took what you wanted,
I watched you become midwife to your mother
at birth and help bring your twin into this world,
this is what I wanted to belong to.

The dark saplings of unmanageable wilderness
that run through your veins mixing with
the gold of ichor, this is how you flick
your wrists and bend whole forests to your will.
The brow that holds a scar from the first fray
you won against your brother and gold-eyed
like the wolves who sing to me every night,
how could I ever resist falling in love with you?
So I took myself from the arms of all my lovers
and gave myself to you. Tell me, Artemis, do
you love me too? Perhaps you do.

Why else when your father sat you
on his throne as an untamable girl child,
and asked you what you wanted,
you told him: 'Give me the moon.'

## An Interlude with Artemis

The night sky is a wolf's mouth today,
and Artemis, bathed in solitude, is on her wild hunt.
I meet her by the silver lake and ask her

about her alone and would she ever give it up for love.
She laughs as she gestures to the exquisite forest.
'What *about* love? I have enough.

How can any one person compare to such splendour?
I traded my duties for belonging to myself,
for this wolf-wild heart was not made to surrender.'

# Modern Apollo and Artemis

Neither of them looked back that last journey walking down the mountains, away from crumbling Olympus.

People give abandonment many names to make themselves feel better. Apollo named his necessary. He called it 'the lesser of two evils'.

Artemis was more brutal. She named hers 'freedom'. In retrospect, that is what it had been for him too. Ever the dutiful son, however, he couldn't call it that in front of his father. Zeus had always preferred Artemis to him, no matter what he sacrificed for his father's love.

Walking away from the toxicity, still glowing in all their gold and silver finery, they had travelled the world, looking for a home together. For the first time, they chose different paths.

For the first time since their birth, Apollo did not know where Artemis was.

Mountains have turned into skyscrapers. The horizon holds an emptiness as the sun has learned how to govern itself. Only the moon still holds her promises. Artemis has made sure of that.

But there is now an endless fury in her bones.

Still the queen of the hunt, still the favourite lover of the forest, but both have altered. She leaves her bow and arrow for switchblades and hunting knives. Tosses in her deer skin and armour for leather jackets and jeans.

Her nymphs have changed too, abandoning the trees for motorcycles, a sharpness to each of their birdlike mouths, mercilessness in their eyes. Years ago, when she had taught them to embrace the darkness, given them direction, trained them to be unafraid of their own woods, which they all carried inside their hearts, she didn't think that it was the smoke of cars, roads and glittering cities she would lead them into.

She had never *wanted* to leave the forest. She had been forced to. When people had stopped paying tribute, she found herself, for the first time, powerless against chain-saws, against men who once she could have turned into stags to be hunted by their own hunting dogs. It made her helpless.

And Artemis was never one to deal with helplessness well. If the fates tried to ignore her, tried to make the world forget her, she would carve her name into them to *force* them to remember; she swore this.

Once, after a kiss too heady, Apollo told a man with eyes the colour of laurels his real name. He regretted the words even before they passed his lips. Trust is far more alien to his kind than it is to Gods.

'Apollo?' the youth drawls in amusement. 'Like the comic books?'

He looks at the beauty he had found so fascinating an hour ago, suddenly being replaced by something else, so young and impossibly fleeting. 'Like the God.'

'Oh.' Clearly thinking this was a game, he touches his lips. 'I've always wanted to kiss a God.'

Apollo is quiet. He feels old and tired and his immortality may just crush him. He removes the hand from his lips and says, 'Perhaps another time.'

Within a minute, the confused man is outside on a cool summer's night, the moon gleaming to show him his way home. The Sun God watches him from his window a while, his eyes slowly turning the forecast of his future like a warm stone in his hand.

It doesn't end well.

But it doesn't end yet. The next day, Apollo finds the man again. This time he brings him home and this time, he asks him to stay.

There are a few Olympian things left about her. Her agelessness for one. Her impatience is another. She does not suffer fools gladly, less so if they are men. She still carries the air of someone completely untouch-able, even though her family's rule long gave way to the newer Gods. The ones who made no mistakes and were pious on a level none of them could have achieved. Not even Hestia, and she was the most pure of them all.

She has found a new way to gain tributes. The nymphs understand this evolution from the forest too. They prowl, silent as cats, cities at night, alleyways, looking for runaway teenagers. Artemis likens each runaway they welcome to Iphigenia, the princess whose father tried to sacrifice her. Leaving behind parents who have betrayed them the material, the maternal and the pa-ternal, each one's eyes telling the kind of story that such young eyes should not hold.

She does not have the power to heal as Apollo does, but she does have the capacity to turn them into something that heals itself.

*Warrior. Hold your monsters close. Turn them into your magic.*

She misses Apollo fiercely but will never tell him that.

Sometimes she thinks of her family.

Sometimes she even wishes them well.

His children are thriving.

Asclepius flourishes in every hospital he has ever been to; he sees him often when he stops trying to heal people. Not that his healing powers are ever the same as they used to be, but it wouldn't matter even if they were. Modern medication is quick, almost as quick as the Gods themselves.

Pamphile's silks flood souks, markets, the homes of kings and the houses of socialites. Who knew when she wove her first ever silken thread, such would be the fate of the fabric.

Aristaeus teaches farmers how to care for their cattle, coax honey from bees, grow the finest grass that feeds the strongest goats. They call him whenever they are in trouble and he appears, sleeves rolled up, ready to get his hands dirty and work hard alongside them. They respect him.

It is almost as good as prayer.

Sometimes, he finds the mouth to the underworld hidden in the city. It is never in the same place twice. Sometimes, it's a basement door no one looks at twice. Other times, it's the phone box covered in graffiti.

Occasionally, he uses it. Goes to find Orpheus wandering happy and free with Eurydice. Of all his children, Orpheus has always had the most understanding of natures and accepting of hearts.

Once, they walked together in the Elysian fields and Orpheus asked his father about his mortal lover. 'Are you happy?'

And Apollo smiled, his face lighting up in a way that would tell anyone watching of his infinite heritage. 'For the first time, yes. Yes, I truly am.'

Artemis once catches three men in an alley trying to overpower a young girl. Her fists clench and she spares no mercy in her swift, harsh punishments.

The girl sobs, thanking her profusely. And this is when Artemis recognises her purpose for the first time away from the forest.

After that, neither Artemis nor her nymphs stay in one city long. Just as all the forests once belonged to her, she has adopted cities too. Cities, like forests, can be sanctuaries. Cities, like forests, can also be a good place to find monsters.

They've adapted too. They wear human skin now. Hide better in plain sight. Know how to smile and laugh, disguise their true intentions. But the Olympian in her sees through it all.

The hunt has changed.
The prey is different.
But Artemis's arrows strike
true all the same.

## Athena and Artemis's Contemporary Manifesto

Come, sisters, let us tell you all the secret
they do not want you to know.

Every woman is both match and spark,
a light for each other from the dark.

When you see them harassing your kind,
this is what you must do.

Join together and descend on them
the way wolves and vultures do.

If they ask you why you did it,
tell them the Goddesses permitted you to.

There is strength in numbers,
this is how armies are made.

And to protect yourself from this world
your friendship in each other is your only aid.

We will help you pry the justice you need
from their cold, cruel fingers, one by one.

We have seen enough of you killed
at the hands of the most brutal of men and Gods
                                    now, *our will* be done.

# Poseidon, God of the Sea

Do not trust the water.
The way it opens, so welcoming,
on a sunny day when the breeze
is all salt water and sweetness.

Waves sweeping gently up
the beach, smoothing the sand,
you would almost forget
what shipwrecks look like.

As if Poseidon was ever known
for his sweet-tempered generosity.
As if whole fleets don't lie on the
sea floor, a testament to his fury.

# Myths about the Water Dispelled

1.

Poseidon's name means Master of Waters,
but the water already had masters
long before Olympian arrogance

declared itself the only true Godhood.
They were the Oceanids –
three thousand Goddesses

who nurtured coral reefs,
planted seaweed on the ocean floor,
helped oysters keep their pearls.

Cultivating life is long deemed woman's work
within the ocean; every fish and mammal
and plant we admire is Oceanid-born.

2.

The water we praise for our existence,
the water that is not full of salt,
but touches our lips, quenches every thirst
is the blessing of Tethys, Titan Goddess
of all fresh water, mother to six thousand Gods.

(If you wonder why Tethys
is rarely mentioned
it is because we take
our fresh waters for granted
and not as an entirely finite source.)

3.

Sailors often pray to Sea Gods, but
it is the Goddesses by whom they are heard.

For Amphitrite had tamed the waters
before Poseidon even knew his first word.

Brizo guides sailors and fishermen to safety
through the storms and their dreams alone.

And Doris is the mother of all the bounty
any sailor, or pirate, or diver ever takes home.

## Poseidon to Zeus

What good is it to own the oceans
when they are only second best to the sky.

What good is it to have invented horses,
when they run at thunder, and at lightning they cry.

It seems there is nothing I do that you will not
outshine just to say you can do it better.

Often, my Godhood feels like a façade next to yours,
like an immaculate treasure chest hidden under wreckage

inside a sea no one will ever discover.
Was it not enough for you that you have

already won what matters most when
our mother chose to save you instead of me.

Perhaps this is why the ocean is the only place for me.
It too knows how to eat whole islands with its jealousy.

# Amphitrite Chides Poseidon

Goddess, Monsteress, Titan Queen,
you didn't discriminate in your misdeeds
so they in turn have become your legacy.

Remember how they transformed to run from you.
Demeter became a mare. Scylla became the Cliffs.
Medusa ran to her temple. Asteria turned into an island.

Is this, then, what it means to be a Sea-God?
A forever drowning of every innocence
to quench your ravenous thirst?

# Amphitrite

I am brine.
I am capacity to calcify
all things holy.

I never saw myself as any less
than the water I knew how to
command with my sisters.

Mortals and Gods know me now
by pity. 'Do you know where your
husband goes?'

I smile and say, 'Always.'
How else do you live with a Kraken
unless you train it to trust you with its life?

I let him think he has more influence
because I know how to live with a blade
and teach it not to make me bleed.

Even Goddesses know the difference
between the patience of a calm sea
and the harrowing wreckage of a storm.

This does not mean he has won.
If he had, I would be broken still.
Instead, I nurture my sharks,

I protect my islands, I build a kingdom
on foundations stronger than his. They never told you
what Delphin King of Dolphins, said to me

so I would agree to marry Poseidon, did they?
'You have ruled the seas for so long,
you know them better than him.

One day his reign will end, and it will
be you who rules in his stead
all of the seas and all of the oceans.'

# Modern-day Sea God(s)

*There are two kinds of people:*
*The ones who merely destroy*
*and the ones who rebuild*
*and restore and recreate,*
*even if it means watching it fall*
*to pieces just to start again.*

He is a sovereign sick of his kingdom. And while most rulers often start hating their crowns, his sickness feels like a bird that is revolted by the sky, a fish tired of the salt water that sustains it.

It is unnatural. It is against the order of everything Olympian ordained, what he has become so used to. But he is tired of mortals who once quaked at the idea of him now tossing their waste into the sea without remorse, for his powers are no longer what they used to be. He has lost count of the poachers' boats he has turned over, the turtles he has freed from nets and plastic.

But a day will come when he cannot watch it any more. A day will come when he looks around at what he once calls home and sees only oil spills and pollution. Where even his beloved friend the dolphin is an endangered thing.

So he puts down his trident inside his coral castle, takes off the sapphire crown and places it on a throne that is slowly being engulfed by seaweed.

Perhaps for some of us, it is easier to leave the thing that nourishes you than face its ending.

Triton has his mother's patience and his father's eyes. But his sense of duty and honour is his own. He shows this by being the kind of man his mother raised as opposed to the man his father refused to bring up. Poseidon, like Zeus, was plagued by prophecies that all ruling Gods were destined to be defeated by their own sons.

While Poseidon is possessively guarded of his throne and his power, his mother teaches Triton that water can only be ruled by a multitude of sea divinities together. This was the ancient way of thinking of the thousands of water Goddesses that had painstakingly crafted the sea, long before the new Gods arrived and ordained it differently.

This is why the news of his father's disappearance did not surprise him. If you insist on shouldering a burden alone simply out of pride, one of two things will happen: you will either succeed in shouldering that burden but compromise everything else ... or that burden will kill you. Still, he worries about the effect his father's leaving may have on his mother and seeks her out. The water was no longer the pure sanctuary it once was, and their powers had long waned.

He finds her already in the throne room holding court with her sisters and all the other remaining blue-skinned, barnacle-covered, seaweed green-haired sea deities. The mood is electric, hushed whispers as they huddle around Amphitrite. The throne room has not been this luminous with voices in years. When she looks up at Triton, she smiles, and he notices that the scales around her face no longer look ancient or dulled with sadness; instead, their phosphorous is glowing. She is glowing.

It is only then he understands: she has been expecting this for a long time. Her divinity has risen to take what is rightfully hers.

His mother has always had a plan, some sleight of hand, some trick to make paths where there were none. His father needed everything to go his way, but she is the master of compromising, creating without giving any of her power away.

Amphitrite understands persuasion and hard work. She has the patience of a sculptor, chipping away at a block of marble to create the smoothness of the statues we so admire. How often has she cajoled Poseidon into listening to her when he is in a hurricane temper. How frequently has she ruled through his words.

While he was away on his jaunts, she spent time preparing for the worst. Plan after plan she drew for what could possibly happen to sea and how to rescue the waters. She had centuries of thoughts, what-ifs and contingencies for if they ever came to be. Her blue fingers had worked out with shells and pebbles, wars and even this – even the mortals forgetting to worship the waters and polluting it.

When it seemed more and more likely that this was the prophecy that was going to come through, she waited for her moment. And now with Poseidon gone, she seized.

She has watched and learned enough over the years to understand that despite being a Sea Goddess, she is a woman. She is used to Gods and mortal men not listening to her. She is too elemental, too vivid for them to understand.

But Triton, with his piercing lagoon-blue eyes, his long mane of moon-silver hair and voice like calm ocean waves on a particularly gentle night, both Gods and mortals will be hypnotised by.

And if there is one way to make mortals care about *anything*, it is by making them invest in a person who cares so much he is happy to bleed for them.

She has carried the saviour of the ocean in her womb. And helped him become his own prophecy.

Now, with her son using the last of his powers to work amongst the mortals with every marine group that is trying to protect the ocean, helping to educate more and more people through every kind of media and governance, she sees the amount of poaching boats lessening in the waters. She notices the amount of oil spills being dealt with faster.

There is still so much work to be done because the oceans and seas are not cleansed yet. But Amphitrite has been waiting for this. Waiting for her husband to leave the oceans so she can prove herself more than a consort – the only one who truly ruled the ocean and ruled it well.

Hera and Amphitrite have this in common. They both know how to win influence despite everyone saying they will not.

They both know how to bide their time, play their cards correctly, and when the moment is right draw blood.

'It will take eras to clear what the mortals have done,' sighs one of her sisters as she releases another dolphin from a plastic bag around its head.

'Olympus was not built in a day either.' Amphitrite lifts her chin with determination, her mirror-like eyes flashing with all of her ancient sagacity. 'Let us begin, shall we?'

# Hestia

Ashen hair, glowing coal.
Fingertips drawn from gold.
Goddess of Hearth,

Goddess of Good Homes,
she knew that Olympus
could never be her own.

She crafted better magic alone
and when Poseidon and Apollo
offered their love, she said no.

It was easier to master the divine flame
than watch her family destroy
each other till this once Godly home

was reduced to nothing but the gold
that bound them together
on this mountain's cold stone.

# Advice from Hestia to Girls

You are not made of paper.
If you were, you would have
turned to ash a long time ago.

You are more. Bone, and muscle,
and beginnings and endings –
evoke that when the world tries
to convince you that you are small.

You are not stone. Your heart is warm,
but seek no homes in other people's chests,
seek no truths there while your own heart,
each throb, reminds you of your true home.

You are not made of paper.
Paper is easy to use and crush,
and you were not made for that.
You were made flame first.

And fire is born knowing
its elemental nature.
It knows the mystic force in shining alone.

# Goddess of Harvest

You have known giving
better than you have known
grieving, but the world forgets.

The best of Gaia's granddaughters,
your fingers both heal
and make flowers burst to fruit.

Amber wheat, bountiful,
you have been mother
not just to Persephone,

but to every child who does not sleep
hungry across this land. Yet, empty coldness
gnaws at your own belly.

For when the harvest season comes,
and the farmers rejoice and pay
a thousand tributes to you,

you are weeping and alone.
For you know well enough
what is coming next.

# Garden Walks with Demeter

Yesterday in my garden, I met Demeter
bringing spring roses to bloom while I was wondering,
'How powerful is my mother's love?'

And she planted a kiss on my forehead and answered,
'When Persephone my child was stolen from me,
I plunged the world into darkness.

Not a single flower could bloom or grow.
When she returned, I brought the whole earth
back to life, everything bathed in sunshine.

That is what a mother's love can do.
It can bring winter in all its fury,
or summer in all its purity.'

# A Friendship: Demeter and Hestia

*When we were girls,*
*we promised each other forevers*
*believing we will never change.*

They are both little girls, caught inside a prison made
by their own blood. They cling to each other in that
darkness for years, raising each other on the promise of
freedom neither of them know will ever happen.

It is there that they learn the true value of leaning on
each other. Where Hera, Poseidon and Hades talk
of vengeance, Demeter and Hestia communicate in
possibilities.

'What will you do when you are free?' Demeter often
wants to know.

'I will warm every corner of the earth,' Hestia says,
shuddering inside this cold prison. 'And you?'

'I will fill fields and fields with flowers so we can play
in the sun.'

The answers are always the same, but they never grow
tired of asking each other the questions.

They never grow tired of helping each other to hope.

Years later, when they are finally freed, they spend all their time together learning newer secrets about their Goddess personalities. Fire becomes Hestia's strength; her role slowly evolves to protect home after home. Harvest and growth become Demeter's domain.

Every victory by one is celebrated by the other. When Demeter first raised a whole field full of wheat to harvest, Hestia hugged her and pulled her into a very un-Goddess-like dance that they both collapsed from, laughing like they were little girls again.

When Hestia mastered her first flames between her fingers and nearly burned down half the forest she was practising in, Demeter hugged her so hard, she could scarcely breathe.

There was no victory too small for celebrations. No story too great to be kept secret between them.

\*

'What you did to her was cruel, it was remorseless and you forget your place, *brother*,' rages Hestia at Zeus, a dangerous glow illuminating her features, her fury impossible to contain.

'If you do not like the way I rule my own domain, you are welcome to leave,' snaps Zeus. He will not be made a fool in his own home, especially by his sisters who he considers lesser divinities.

Hestia watches the downcast Demeter hold her middle where her child was growing and raise her head high. 'We shall both leave then.' Demeter steps forward, her rage making every one of Hera's roses wither to nothingness. 'I would rather my child be safe than be here.'

Hestia takes her sister's hand and glares at Zeus with her. 'Olympus will fall under you.'

They leave together, set up homes in the mortal world.

True to their words, neither of them ever returns.

\*

Kore is a beautiful child in every way. Demeter and Hestia raise her to grow flowers, and dance in the sunshine, and always have warmth – things they never had as little girls.

Demeter asks Hestia one evening as the Goddess of the Hearth slowly stokes the fire in their dear little fireplace, 'What if she leaves?'

Hestia pauses, and puts the poker down. 'Then we let her go.'

'What if I can't?' asks Demeter, and Hestia sees the fear in her eyes.

'Then I will help you learn.' Hestia hugs her sister fiercely with the reassurance she knows is needed.

*

Kore does leave. Demeter falls apart. Falls into denial. Grief rots the flowers, the fruits, the world.

Hestia comforts and cares.

Hestia rebuilds and replenishes.

Hestia holds and heals.

Demeter's grief causes her to wither and wilt and become a quarter of the Goddess she was.

Hestia goes into the underworld, to reason with Kore who now calls herself Persephone.

Kore visits them. She is no longer the soft, dark-haired child who left them, but the redheaded, majestic Queen of Hell who insists on being called Persephone.

Demeter's face is white with rage, but Hestia places a hand on her arm to stop her.

Quiet, controlled, Demeter asks, 'How could you abandon me this way?'

Persephone eyes her mother wryly. 'Would you have let me go any other way?'

For a second there is silence, other than the wood that crackles in the fireplace.

'No,' says Demeter finally. 'No, I wouldn't.'

Persephone settles back. 'Now you know.'

They sit quietly for the rest of their time together, until it is time for Persephone to go.

*

'She's a silly little girl.'

'She's a woman in love and is loved in return. That is a powerful thing.'

'Love means nothing.'

'Love, dear sister, is everything.'

Demeter looks at her sister hard. 'How would you know? You have never loved anyone in your life.'

Hestia smiles serenely, 'Not in that way, no. And I never will. But I do have someone I have loved enough to leave family and home for.'

'Who?' demands Demeter.

'You.'

*

Every love does not have to be made of desire.
Some loves are kept for the people
who stand by you through everything.
Some soulmates are sisters not lovers.
Some loves are for those who give you hope.
And some for the strength, for wisdom, for dreams.

## Demeter to Hades
(A Mother's Fury)

You smell of death.
Everything about you
is an endless goodbye.

I will give this union no blessings.
Not when even your presence
will harm my fae daughter.

She is a child of flora,
of fauna, of fruit,
too gentle for your hell.

You overestimate yourself here,
in the land of the harvest,
daring to return to ask

me for my most precious thing,
what you stole. Beware, King of Death,
for I am Queen of the Living,

and this deified land's roots
will hold you forever in place
if I say a word to will it.

Give me my girl back,
now, today, and I promise
no harm will come to you.

# Persephone to Demeter

Do you remember what happened
the first time I touched a pomegranate shrub?
Instead of bursting to a full red fruit,
it wilted and mottled under my fingers
until you snatched it and brought it back to life.

We both knew in that moment,
I nurtured something in my chest you
couldn't bring yourself to love.
So you kept me hidden, deep in a forest
where no one could find me,

the darkness an ugliness festering
under this, my pretty nymph skin.
But, Mama, he found me. He saw me
nourish this beast in the woods,
fell in love with the part of me that
no one else could, promised me a land where

I could be a queen and not another version of you,
a place where I could unleash my flaws and fury
without having to disappoint you. They told you
they could bring me back to you, to pacify your anger,
so you could bring back the spring.

They needed you to remind the birds to sing,
but, Mama, you gave birth to a girl
who knows her own mind. He didn't snatch me
and take me to hell. I went there because
I wanted a queendom destined to be mine.

# Hades to Persephone

I sensed you before I saw you.
The sugar flavour of meadow wrapped
nectar in the air, and my eyes searched
for its source, your face the essence

of what I had been waiting for
all those cold and lonely years
my family had made me the guardian
of Elysian and hell, until you stepped

into my world like a galaxy bursting
in front of an astronomer's telescope.
Tell me, with all those speckles
on your skin did anyone tell you that

you are a constellation, waiting to be loved
and explored? Did the bumbling River-Gods
who tried to court you ever understand
that you were destined for so much more?

I saw you, Spring Goddess, restless in your loneliness,
pulling at crimson flowers to watch them die,
wondering if immortality was worth anything
if you were powerless to have any control

over your fate or your destiny. Come now,
tell the truth. I saw you rattle at the invisible
chains of smother, of boredom, of too
much comfort.

Let me give you the challenges
you need: the mastery over
your own fortunes
and the legacy of a queen.

Allow me the privilege to be the darkness
behind your shining star, become the queen
of my kingdom of dead and show those who did not
understand you for the Goddess you really are.

## Persephone to Hades

You are still the kindest thing
that ever happened to me,
even if that is not how our tale is told.

Where everyone told me I was destined
to be a forgotten Goddess who nurtured
flowers and fostered golden meadows,

you saw how the ichor in my blood
yearned for its own throne.
You showed me

how our love can transform
the darkest, coldest realm
into the happiest of homes.

# Persephone to Theseus and Pirithous

Be wary if you have come here
with hearts full of lies,
eels instead of tongues,
desecration in your eyes.

Heroes and villains all end
in the shadows of the same Hades
you have so arrogantly penetrated,
hoping to steal a Goddess from her God.

Styx will not stop you.
Cerberus will not kill you.
Hecate will turn a blind eye.
Tartarus will simply smile at you.

They all know what you forget,
that not a soul mentions the name Persephone here.
Not because she is forgotten or too small
but because she is the terror that makes fear swell.

Once daughter of the Goddess of Harvest,
Once Goddess of the Spring,
now the proud dread queen
of all hell.

# Persephone and Hades, After

Being in the business of death means that you never actually go out of business. For until a cure for mortality is invented, the underworld will always be full of souls and Hades will always be king.

If he had known this when his brothers tricked him into being King of the Underworld while they took the sky and the sea, he would not have spent millennia brooding about it.

His immortality and his kingdom both secure, and thousands of underlings to watch over the dead, the fields of Asphodel and Elysian, Tartarus and the banks of the river Styx, he has finally earned time to do what he always wanted to do.

*

Persephone still comes home to her mother; their relationship has improved over the centuries, but she misses her husband more each time she has to leave him.

Even now, sitting across from her mother and aunt in their comfortable red armchairs, in the warm glow of the fire, she misses the blue flames of Styx, the walks through Elysian and Asphodel, Hecate's palace, and even more than all of that, she misses her role as Queen of the Dead.

Forever torn between her role of bringing life into the flora and fauna of the world and ruling over the kingdom of hellfire, she is secretly glad that the days of spring are reducing so that she can be with Hades.

She says nothing of this to her mother, however.

She knows how sad it makes her mother to still have to say goodbye to her daughter every year.

Her mother's uncompromising love is also why Persephone will never have children. She couldn't bear to love someone like this.

\*

The shelter is unlike any shelter ever seen before. For one, it is its own island. Canopies of trees, golden beaches, fields and grass, and a large shelter made of bricklike material with thousands of comfortable dog beds.

Secondly, it is run by the strangest people anyone has ever seen, and they are rarely seen at all. So many television crews have found their way onto the land and only been greeted by its sole residents, very happy and playful dogs. Once in a while they see a pale man in black. Or a striking maiden with long red hair. But as soon as they try to approach them, they are gone.

When she returns, everything is much the same, for what could possibly change exponentially in the land of the dead? She stops at Hecate's palace for a long conversation. She smiles at Charon who bows to her, and gives Thanatos a hug, the only one he ever allows to do so. These are the parts of her that are the joyful child-like goddess of spring.

Then she walks into her own palace and greets her husband with the kind of gentle, soul-searching kiss that comes after so long apart. The kind which says 'I missed you, I love you, I am so relieved to be home.' They go together to their throne room, regal, beautiful, eternal.

Persephone sits by Hades's side, on a throne made of skulls intertwined with black roses. He looks over and takes her hand, interlaces it with his and kisses it, his usually cold eyes warm.

He keeps his tenderness for her, she knows this; to others, he is the cold, unfeeling dread lord of the vast underworld – feared, incapable of love or emotion, executer of punishments that last eternities, never ever to be crossed.

But she knows something about him that no one else knows. That when the day is over, and the deeds of all the dead settled, they will go to their island for a long walk, surrounded by the new dogs Hades has rescued while Persephone has been away and he will introduce them all by name to her. She will smile and pet them all on the head, because she understands his love for dogs so well. They are loyal in a way their Olympian family has never been to them, a way for them to know truly unconditional love widely and well.

Even the dread King and Queen of the Underworld make gentle attempts at compassion in a world that is slowly forgetting how to burn the flames of kindness forever.

# The Messenger, the Trickster,
# Guide of the Dead

Let there be eloquence.
Let there be a God

who toys with the metaphysical
for capricious reasons and nothing more.

Call him thief and messenger,
trickster and guide,

watch him wear all these names
with equal pride.

Let there be a paradox.
Let there be a half-devil

who challenges us all
on our small human notions

of what is truly good and if
what is good can also then be evil.

Fleet-footed, silver-tongued prince
who saw the universe in a day,

what do you keep searching for
which does not let you stay?

# The Life of Every Party

*The problem is preferring crimson to gold.*
He is like his mother. Trusting.
Trusting is best left to mortals,
not to Gods, never to Gods.

Hermes tries to teach him this.
Apollo tells him how he is twice born.
But no one tells him of the madness
because they fear their own sanity gone.

Something about this boy-God
invokes unspeakable dark fears
as much as it invokes the need
for heady wine and happy tears.

So they send him away, let him travel the earth
until he becomes hero everywhere he goes.
When they summon him back
his half-human is youthful,

yet his Godhood seems
so bone-chillingly old.
Mortals tell stories better than Gods do,
and the truth has turned him cold.

As he watches his family
dissolve into madness and fold,
he smiles and thinks to himself:
*The answer is preferring crimson to gold.*

## Conversations Between Hermes and Dionysus

*'Do you miss it?'*

*'Miss where?'*

*'Olympus. Being a God.'*

*'Sometimes. When the moon is full enough to look like a silver coin. When my feet ache like a mortal's after running for a time too short. You?'*

*'No. Never.'*

*'You were always the most human one of us.'*

Hermes is a God of both. Every bad choice, and clever one. Mischief made, and goodness done. Of thieves and all of those nights fuelled by rum and wit and laughter, and those same midnights trailed in mistakes but unforgettable memories.

Dionysus is the God of Wine, of frenzy, of night after night of hedonistic parties. Being with him is a slow, passion-filled descent into madness. The danger of becoming a slave to every one of your own vices and not recognising what you have done until it is too late.

Hedonism and wit go well together.

As far as Gods will ever go, it is no surprise that they are both brothers and best friends.

*'Are you lonely?'*

*'Never. Are you?'*

*'Without her? Always.'*

Ariadne was everything he did not merit but everything he needed. Graceful till the end, dancing joy into his life, the only one who knew how to bring the truest of smiles to his face, not even his maenads knew how to do that. She was not beautiful but she was grounded and she carried the look of someone who had known sorrow and thus knew kindness. There was something so human about her. Something that called to the crimson in his blood that mixed with the ichor.

When she was killed, he did everything a God shouldn't. He reacted with the rage of a man. He shouted curses at his own father, he ripped open a hole in the ground, descended into the underworld, fought Thanatos, almost wrestled Hades to the ground and demanded her back.

He was no Orpheus. He had no lyre, no singing voice, but he had something more dangerous, more terrifying: the promise of a madness so profound that even Hades would lose control of his kingdom.

Many had tried before him, but it took a God with mortal blood to bring the chthonic deities to their knees, and Hermes, who was the only Olympian with free passage into the underworld, had howled with laughter at the sight of the usually gentle-faced Dionysus hold the entire kingdom of the dead hostage over the fate of his wife.

*'Is there anyone you once loved?'*

*'Me? No.'*

*'Ah.'*

*'You are smiling.'*

*'I can finally see why they call you the God of Lies.'*

Aphrodite.

Daeira.

Peitho. Peitho. *Peitho.*

Even now he wondered where she was. She made him uncomfortable, tested him, saw him for what he was. She was constantly slipping through his fingers like sand, she had no love for his capriciousness nor worship of his Olympian heritage. She treated him as an equal. It was infuriating to his arrogance, and on more than one occasion he thought he had got the better of her, but she was always one step ahead of him. Their love was a constant sparring contest, riddled in puzzles and mazes and good debates. Always an adventure.

Of course, he married her. Who else could he ever marry?

And, of course, she left him.

He had expected nothing less. He was not the kind to settle down and neither was she.

*'One day, you will tire of the constant running.'*

*'Perhaps. But that day is not today. And today the wine is flowing, the night is warm, the moon is full and we are Gods again.'*

# 4. A Mortal Interlude

Persephone, grant me the foresight to know when I must let go my old life to start anew.

Artemis, grant me the strength of your spine when you helped deliver Apollo, your own twin.

Athena, grant me the solidarity in your sinews for which you were born in all of your armour.

Aphrodite, grant me the kind of heart that always follows my passions true.

Amphitrite, grant me the wish to never fall out of love with the sea or the glisten of its waters.

Demeter, grant me the love I need to nurture and to foster.

Hestia, grant me warmth, so that I can aid those in pain, show them how to find their way home.

And Hera, grant me your fury, so I can remind my enemies I am not the weakness they perceive, I am the oncoming storm, I am war.

'Many who have learned from Hesiod the countless names of gods and monsters never understand than night and day are one.'

—*Heraclitus, 35, Fragments,*

# Monster Mine

I've been interviewing
monsters lately.

The sirens inform me
that they were just
doing their jobs.

And the Hydra tells me
she still doesn't know
what she did wrong.

The Stymphalian birds
said they only wanted
to protect where they belonged.

It is a worrying thought
that the monsters may actually
have been heroically fighting

to protect what was theirs
from invaders and
against the odds.

That we may need monsters.
What else will ever help us
make sense of the Gods?

## Asterion

Tell no one how a sister crept through night no longer sacred, across an island once loved, now cursed by Poseidon. Tell no one how under a palace built by a King, there lived a bull-headed boy who only wanted his mother. That the bellows were cries, his horns made to be adorned with marigold garlands his sister created, yet instead around his neck he wore cold cruel chains. Do not tell anyone how they lashed him and broke him until everything gentle in him was gone. A soft-hearted sister was no match in the end for a King's revenge, as she watched the teenage star-named brother disappear and instead in his place stood the Minotaur. Take this secret to the grave, Ariadne, sweet sister, tell no one of the love in his chest you thought would free him from his destiny. Kings and Gods need monsters to descend into madness so they can kill them to be worshiped and adored.

## Athena to Medusa

I'll make you a trade, your beauty for stone,
Your sea-beloved tresses for venom-filled snakes,
your innocent doe eyes for frigid gaze.

The sea is in the habit of ravishing
what does not belong to him,
taking without consideration.

But, sweet girl, I promise you,
I will not allow this to be your ruin.
You are sacred, one of my own.

And no cruel chaos will devour you again,
choose terror over maiden,
relinquish your human.

And I will turn you into a Goddess
in your own right, a deity of monsters,
a myth that will scare men for all the years
and their seasons.

# Echidna to Typhon

You are a loud desecration.
A thing built to destroy all that is sacred.

Mother Earth's most fearsome weapon,
created to bring the Olympians to their knees.

Ten thousand years you waged battles against them,
and still you brought home no glory.

I remember you then. Fire-eyed and viper smile,
lava dripping from your teeth, did they ask you,

Typhon, what you wanted? Did they ask you
what you needed your purpose to be?

Loyal son and savage beast, a paradox in
the same body. You met me here,

in the innermost sanctum of hell.
Like you, I too was punished for being created

hideous, a being of fear that was a wholly
necessary thing, Yet no one wanted to admit

me a necessity. Just like no one wanted to admit
your allegiance to your family. Your loyalty

to me is the most treasured thing I love
about you. This dichotomy of being a beast

who can love his wife in such an unbeastlike way
and treasure and raise his children too.

# Scylla

Sweet-mouthed, silver-skinned,
and the sea's lullabies in your smile,

you never meant to be a siren,
you didn't try to catch Poseidon's eye.

Nymphs are trinkets in the hands of Gods,
toys from a celestial nursery,

meant to be played with and forgotten.
At least this is the case for those who are lucky.

You, however, were too pretty for your own good
so instead you kept his attention.

What happens when a God stays too long
with something that should be a trifling affection?

In his hurry to hide you from his God-wife,
you ended up a botched experiment.

You were supposed to turn into cliffs;
instead he took your limbs and gave you serpents,

four dogs from your waist, and a hunger
that was apocalyptic devastation.

A man made you a deep sea monster,
so you flung yourself into the ocean

and attacked ship after ship of men,
making each one your victim.

At least you had Charybdis,
a friend with the same afflictions,

and together you became
the rock and the hard place,

the devil and the deep blue sea,
a fable about choices

Gods and monsters,
the ugly truth about

the beings we worship
and claim to know so well.

# Gorgon (A Letter to the Patriarchy)

If a woman does not fit the shape
of what you think a woman should,

if a woman is not obedient,
does not see things the way you do,

if a woman is too independent
to need anything more than herself,

does she automatically become
a threat filled with such terror to you?

Did her tresses turn into red snakes
because she dared to refuse you?

Did the dulcet voice become unbearable cries
because you couldn't stand to hear her laugh?

Did her gaze turn you to stone
because she was so completely unafraid?

Perhaps the truth about Gorgons
is they are just women,

women who do not bend to the world
or fit into the narrow mould you want them too.

Maybe that's why you demonised them,
turned them into monsters,

because you think monsters are easier
to understand than women who say no to you.

## Lamia to Scylla

What is the punishment for catching the eye of a God?

A wreckage of a human life, a destiny repeated,
a spell of madness, and every ivory bone defeated.

Once a queen of Libya, once a nymph fair,
mortal daughter and granddaughter of Gods,

who knew how close our fates would fare.
One of us would murder her own children,

in a fit of madness I cannot remember.
The other would spurn the advances of a God

who was marked to be loved by another.
One of us was cast into insomnia and grief.

And the other was turned into a sea fiend
by a Goddess scorned who took no pity.

At least I was gifted my monstrous fate
by the God who loved me to stop all the mockery.

He handed me fangs as a weapon, the power
to terrify anything that ever turned on me.

We are battle-born now, daughter, you to the sea
and I serpent-like snake through this land.

They say I devour children, and that I am a whore,
but they speak in hushed whispers and no one is laugh-
ing any more.

# The Erinyes: Vengeance-skinned Fury

You do not know sacred until you lose your purpose.
Then sacred becomes anything that reminds you

of what you once called home. Even if home is
the inner sanctum of hell itself. You were

rough-skinned girls, wing-backed and vengeance born,
they couldn't define you so they ran from you.

Daughters of Ouranos's blood and rage, hungry things
that could detect the sin of the darkest hearts.

You are a thing so elemental, even Zeus was afraid.
One day, you would come after him, set him ablaze,

and even though it was tempting, and what he did
to those girls made the scream bubble in your chest,

you knew one day he would finish, his reign would end.
So now the Gods are dead and nothing holds you back,

you stare down at this planet full of monstrous men
escaping punishment, spread your ancient wings,

crick your necks and get yourself ready for a new hunt.
It is time to craft sacred again, and this time,

you will do it with the blood of men who hurt women
and children and show absolutely no remorse for their
acts.

# 5. A Mortal Interlude: To the Poets

I know why you did it.
Turned your own wounds
into the stories of Gods
and heroes; it's easier to picture
the pain that way, turn it sweet,
so strangers and even loved ones
who hear you do not realise
that when you say, this is the way
Zeus betrayed Hera, you are talking
about how your first love betrayed you
and each of Hercules's twelve labours
is penance you paid for hurting people.
The truth is too painful to admit.
It is digging bodies from a ground
so unhallowed you hesitate
to call it memory. It's better to touch it
through a veneer of sacred stories.

Name is Achilles. Call it Helen.
Christen it Megara. Or Patroclus.
As long as it makes you feel
holy, less human, less sullied.

At least, it cannot harm you that way.

*The Mortals*

'Take courage, my heart: you have been through worse than this.'

—Homer, *The Odyssey 20:18*

# Defy a God

Do it.
Do it for every girl
and boy who fell
prey to a Zeus.
Or a Poseidon.
Or was called 'wreckage'
instead of 'human'.

Face him,
face him and tell him
how you are still mighty,
turn the full stops
in his heroic tales
into commas where
they tell *your* story.

Remind him
Remind him
how you are still valid,
still majestic
despite his best attempts
at your ruin.

# Danaë, Mother of Perseus

There is a wounding here. A winding, a weathering, my story has been twisted into something it has not. A litany of half-truths follow me wherever I go. *She is the daughter of a feckless king who tossed her and her newborn in a box into the sea.* This is the truth. *She was Zeus's lover.* This is false. *He made her with child as golden rain.* This is true. *She worshipped him and swore she would never love another.* This is false. *She was chosen by the Storm Bringer.* This is true. *She did not love the child he gave her.* This is false. *She loved a fisherman.* This is true. *She was the whore who tempted his king brother.* This is false. *She bore a son who would murder her father.* This is true. *She was glad for his death and danced when she heard of the murder.* This is false.

*I terrified kings.* This is true. *I carved a life out of a destiny that was against me.* This is true. *I turned my tragedy into an asset.* This is true. *I am remembered as a vessel to a hero as opposed to the catalyst the Gods depended upon.* This is true. This is true. This is true.

# Andromeda, Princess of Ethiopia, Wife of Perseus

What they will tell you ...

Once upon a time, a princess was naked and chained to cruel rocks, a sacrifice to a sea monster sent by Poseidon until a son of Zeus would come and save her. And they would fall in love and become constellations together in the night sky.

*A consort. A prop. An ornament to glorify a man's story.*

This is what they will forget ...

She was an April before him already. Bosom full of spring, every intention honed in the abrupt nature of wildflowers. At night, as the moonlight braided her thick onyx hair, she taught herself the art of kindness by watching over the dust-covered city. By day, she waited for the skies to turn pink before disappearing in a beggar's garb into a city that was wounded and crying out, the voices of hunger sounding the same no matter where she went. Every starving child she handed food to, every alm she passed to a beggar, she knew there were a dozen more she had not helped, and this weighed heavy on her.

*A saviour. A solace. An instrument to aid the poor.*

This is what they do not know …

The palace was equal measures of beauty and hypocrisy. Beautiful, wealthy women and girls who pretended they loved their golden cages in an assortment of painful ways. Some tormented serving girls. Some tormented each other by stealing the other's lovers. Embracing a prison becomes easier if you grow as cold as the metal that controls your freedom. They bow their heads when they see her, but she hears the whispers sharp as poniards lift in the air and pierce her ears. *There is a knowing in her*, she hears them say, *that makes her untamable.* She has known since she was a child that she is observant in a way that makes them uncomfortable.

*A story. A princess. At the mercy of her parents.*

*My daughter is the finest of all our jewels*, boasts her mother, her third glass of wine teetering in her hand. *More exquisite than any woman in all the land. She makes the Nereids look hideous in her wake.* Outside, the sea roars, and the palace walls tremble, as if they know a great folly has been made.

*A challenge. A pawn. A sacrifice to be made.*

They say when the message from Poseidon came in the form of a great sea storm, her father cried. He fell to his knees and begged every God in the sky. He said he would give up anything for her. *Anything*, other than his kingdom. In the end, the skies were empty, and his throat dry. So she made the decision for them. She would rather be dead than watch her city burn, than listen to children cry.

*A damsel. A monster. A hero in the making.*

When she was seven years old, her tutor asked her what a queen's role was. Her answer was laughed at, scorned and refused, for she said that a queen's role was 'Be just. Have courage. And rule.'

'Queens cannot rule. They can only bear sons who will.'

*We can,* whispered a voice in her head. *Oh, but we can.*

*A rock. A survivor. A constellation soon to grace the sky.*

This is what they do not want you to know for they cannot believe a princess can face Cetus. Surely women cannot be shrewd enough to know his weakness was inside his many-fanged mouth, his eyeless head. They underestimate what a woman can do when she has to survive. Grab a sword, visit a witch, even learn the secrets that will destroy a monster well. How a night-skinned princess left as sacrifice on a rock, without a single Olympian gift to save her, could face a primordial thing so ancient and win with only her wits.

The rest of the story is written in stars if you watch them closely as they swivel and swell. They will tell you about Andromeda. Constellation. Hero. Queen who saved her city and herself.

## Penelope, Wife of Odysseus

They call me loyal,
the antithesis of Helen.

Where she is ruination,
I am purification.

But it is not my face that will set
a thousand ships to sail.

*You are not beautiful*, says my mother.
*Make this your virtue instead of your deficiency.*

I remind myself of this on the docks,
watching my husband's warship leave,

and when I must raise our son alone
while ruling Ithaca without being King.

Even when I hear the war has ended,
yet for year after year, he does not come home.

The bards sing of his exploits as I stand alone –
cunning Odysseus, brave Odysseus –

while they are only able to feed themselves
from food and water my reign provided

and name me an addendum to a hero's tale.
They whisper about the Goddesses you are with

and laugh behind my back,
while to cope, I sew, I mother, I rule.

When he finally comes home,
he butchers brutish suitors to protect my honour

without considering how I've evaded them
for ten years with only my wits and shrouds.

And while he reclaims his throne,
hero once again, no one asks the question:

if a wife is only measured a good wife
by how faithful she has been,
then what makes the gauge of a good husband?

## Argos, Dog of Odysseus

It wasn't always this way. Once, I had a master who loved me, walked with me across these quieter lands. And then one day, he left. No one told me why. People don't tell dogs such things for they think we do not understand, but we grieve when we lose our best friends too.

So I aged, alone. My fur went grey, my eyes rheumy. I was no longer the tracking dog my master once knew.

But I kept myself alive, just to see him one last time, for I knew he would return home no matter what anyone said. I just wanted to hear him say I was a good dog as he did when I was a pup running along the sandy beach of Ithaca, bringing him back fish and birds I had caught in my mouth.

Everyone forgot me after he's gone. I became a small ghost in the home I was supposed to protect. The mistress was too busy running a kingdom, the master's son was too young for a hunting dog, and I found myself without the purpose to which I was born.

I suppose that is why when my master returned, I was so old, mangy and sitting neglected on piles of manure.

I wagged my tail, smiled so wide, let him know I was there. I was too weak to stand on my legs, but he was

so close, I could not understand he walked past me as though he did not care.

Had I been a bad dog? Did I do something wrong? Hope left me as my heart broke, and I sadly rested my head between my paws and closed my eyes a final time. I was alone without a soul to pat my head and asssure me everything would be fine.

When my eyes opened again, two men stood before me. One shone bright, bright like the sun, but the other was darkness itself. He wore a long coat and had a crown of onyx upon his head, yet his voice was clear and true. I lifted my head wearily, and pricked my ears and tried to understand what they were saying, but I could not. Humans didn't speak in tongues easy for dogs to understand; we only understood their emotions and some of their thoughts.

When the man with the onyx crown knelt before me and patted my head, I quickly realised he was not a man at all, but a God. 'Argos does not suit you. I think I will call you Cerberus.'

As soon as the words left his pale lips, I felt my ancient body shake. At first, I was afraid, but the God's reassuring eyes did not leave mine, and that made me brave.

Suddenly I was young, a giant and two more heads that looked as fearsome as the Nemean lion. My paws were the size of small lakes, the strength of a thousand dogs in my bones.

The God, much smaller than me now, looked up at me, smiled tranquilly and patted my front paw. 'Good boy.'

My new master was kind to me. He had many dogs and the underworld was wonderful to explore with my new friends as we always had so much time.

The master and mistress both took me for walks, and although there are no beaches here, the fields of Asphodel were strewn with white flowers and glades of grass, and even a dome that pretended it was the bluest of skies, bluer than my old master's home in Ithaca. But the best thing ever was that my new master never ever forgot to give me a pat or call me a good boy.

And I would smile so widely with all three of my mouths and thump my serpent tail, before I returned to guarding the mouth of hell.

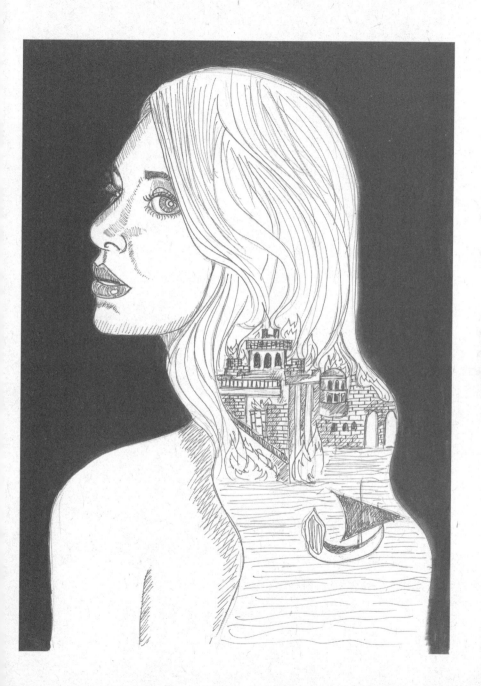

# Helen

To the men who forgot
I am half God before
I am a woman,

did you really believe
that I would not choose
freedom, sky-flavoured

and sea-beloved over
the fickle prison
you kept me in?

Did you really think
I would not be golden sand
slipping through your fingers?

That once wed
you could forget me
until I was needed?

Did you forget
whose divine blood
it is that runs through my veins?

Did it not strike you,
Theseus, Menelaus,
Agamemnon,

Achilles,
and yes,
even you, Paris,
that I would
always belong
to myself first,

and that is
the only reason
I would run?

Did you think that if you trapped
the Storm Bringer's daughter
into a life of subservience

there would be no consequences?
That you, and everything
you love, would not burn?

## Briseis Remembers

I watched fire devour my entire city.
The kind oak trees that once gave me shade
alight. The place my parents first met
consumed by cruel amber flames.
The elegant bones of every temple
I had worshipped in torn asunder by fire,
every home, every shop, everything.
Oh God, they burned everything.
They killed our fathers and our brothers
then tore our homes asunder.
We can still hear them screaming
at night when we see the flames dance.
We can hear our families, our home
screaming. When I was little
I asked my nurse-maid,
'How does a girl become a shadow?'
And she told me, looking out
to where the black ships stood
and men beat at the walls of my horse
with weapons and war cries,
'When we watch everything burn
that is how girls become shadows.'
But she was wrong. It wasn't just
watching the burning, it was *becoming*
the burning that made a girl a shadow.
I watched fire devour everything I loved.
And prayed to a God who never came.
That, *that* is how a girl becomes a shadow.

# Hecuba, Wife of Priam, Mother of Paris

I found the body of my last son
on the same golden beach
where he once played as a boy,
killed by greedy hands
that threw him to a watery end.

I make no bones, no apologies
for what I did next. I know
the world prefers women soft,
only because it does not
wish to know what happens

when we swallow rage and war
for so many years it becomes
no different from our names.
Brutal women are unafraid
to take blood for blood,

to haunt the very sinews
of those who steal our families.
I exacted my revenge,
took an eye for an eye,
stole from Polymestor

the way he had stolen
from Polydorus,
then ran to give myself

to the same sea that carried
my child, my child,

my last born child.

But the Gods had other
plans for me. I felt the fur
grow first, my sobs turn to howls,
my hands now paws.
I now spend eternity as a dog.

Perhaps they thought I would be unhappy
that they had brought a savage woman
to heel, but Hecate, the Goddess I am
bound to, is kinder than they will ever see.
She understands me and treats me well.

I in turn follow her between
heaven and hell.
But sometimes
I think of the children
I never got to bury and wonder,

could I still call myself a mother
of princes and princesses,
of warriors and priestesses,

when our kingdom is ash
and every single child

I once bore,
loved and raised
has become
equal parts
dust and death?

## Iphigenia, Daughter of Agamemnon

*When I was a child, I loved rainbows.*

The way the sun scrambled into the sky after the rain to shine through the prisms of blue, make violet, indigo, blue, green – I tried to catch them between my small fingers but ended up empty-handed. Still, I never stopped trying.

Back then, I was my father's favourite. He brought home dresses as turquoise as the ocean's lagoons and sat me on his knee to tell me of the glittering future he saw for me.

But I did not want glitter, I just wanted to make him happy. So I nodded along to every word he said, my large eyes glowing for the only man who I knew would never betray me.

When my mother tells me of Achilles the first time, my cheeks redden, however it is not out of shyness, but because I am afraid. I am scarcely old enough to consider the idea, let alone old enough to even know what it means to be a wife.

But my father is determined, and I have never once let him down. I will not break his heart to salvage my own.

My wedding dress is unusual. It holds the vivaciousness of violets, the hues of the rivers, every shade of forest you can imagine. My father has not spared any expense. I smooth the fabric against my skin with my fingers as my mother helps me arrange it. *They will tell stories about your wedding day. Even the Gods will be in attendance to bless your union.*

But when the soldiers come for me, my mouth goes dry. I have yet to meet Achilles, and even my father has not yet appeared to say goodbye.

At least they made the altar pretty.

Pure white marble, in a crimson tent awaits the resting of my head. It takes me a second to understand what is happening. This has happened to girls from other families, women whisper of it all the time. But never mine. I had always been confident of my father's love for me, his protection of me. My heart thuds in my chest as I look around to seek my father's eyes. When I find him, he cannot look at me. His usually sturdy voice breaks as he says, 'If you do not do this, the Goddess Artemis will not allow our ships to sail.'

My fists clench at the betrayal, at the fact that he thought I would not do this without being tricked, that I would not try to save his honour even though I was his kin. Then my mind whirls at why he is doing this. To go and wage a war that is not even his, that he can choose not to be a part of. Rage and alarm have an unusual flow together: one burns red hot whilst the other is as cold as the underworld.

'Did you mistake the glitter of my blood for the glitter of my future, father?' I asked him, trying to make him look at me. He looks at the floor, not answering.

'You can have my life. On one condition,' I said softly. 'If I am to die, it is you who must take my life.'

For the first time in my life, I saw fear in the eyes of the great Agamemnon. His sword hand shook as I offer my throat. Still, he does not fall to his knees and beg forgiveness as I had hoped. I close my eyes and resign myself to this fate. Perhaps a world where a father can kill a beloved daughter for a war is not a good world to be a part of after all.

But instead of feeling the cruel, cold strike of a sword against my throat, I sense my body slowly disintegrate. I open my eyes to see I am no longer at any altar, my father has disappeared and I am surrounded by the colours I have always loved since I was a child.

Later, I learn Artemis has been watching. She saw courage in me, my honour and the need to control my own destiny. It was she who took me in her arms, bathed me in ambrosia and transformed me into Iris, rainbow maiden, messenger to the Gods and Titans alike.

*When I was a child, I loved rainbows.*

*Now I paint them with my fingers into the sky all the time.*

# Megara Laments from the Underworld

How does one magic the brutality of murder into poetry? Ovid made it all look so pretty, truly. Turn a picture where murder of innocents is just a footnote in a hero's story. Make the violence into a necessity. Turn the victims into an instrument to aid a plot. Blame a Goddess for her pettiness and cruel nature, and a God for his amorousness. Call it madness, and defend him and say he paid his penance. Ask his wife, a mere woman after all, what did you expect if you were going to wed a hero. How did you not know he could do this? Did you not know him well enough then, that he could be like this? Did you sneer at him once too often? Why didn't you leave if he did this to you before? What did you expect other than storms, his eyes filled with bloodlust as he snapped the neck of you and yours? Are you sure you didn't provoke him? Are you sure you aren't somehow to blame? Are you sure it wasn't you who anguished him into doing this terrible thing we dare not name?

# Hippolyta Speaks to the Gods

Bless this world in lifeblood.
Bless it with the stories
of the women who bled with me.
Who did not have a belt of immortality.
Who followed me into battle,
with nothing but love for each other and me.
Bless it with the sisterhood
it may never see again.

Bless it with a story where
this land, made of women
and wanton wilderness is left untouched.
We still sing songs and dance together,
fashion armour, put flower crowns
in each other's hair, where no one but
us have a say, where at full moon
we all bleed together.

Bring me back to this,
where we can still watch our daughters grow.
Love each other the same way.
Where the moonlight meets morbid
and they call magic by its name.
This is how it should be.
An eternity crafted from our
own bonds and secret games.

For what good is it to be the daughter
of the vicious God of War?
What good is it to be the leader
of a legendary tribe of women
who do not bow and do not break,
If the myth still ends this way?

With the same message every time:
'You are powerful. You are revered.
But still you will meet your end
At the hands of men.'

# Io Explains Recovery to Europa

Steal normal away from normal. Turn tragedy on its head. When the nightmares come, grit your teeth but do not scream. Glare into the skies every morning, promise yourself, 'This is not the end of you, this is not the end of you, this is not the end of you.' Bathe with ice-cold water of the ocean just to feel something again. Trauma isn't going to win today. Remember how Daphne turned into the laurel tree? This is what you must do too. Form your own roots, feed from the earth that still loves you. Remember how. Take the day one cautious step at a time. Remember how fearless tastes. Remember how your grandmother told you 'always prepare for the worst of situations by being the best of yourself'. Try not to think how the worst-case scenario will now be everyday in these once hallowed halls. Your father could be a River God, an emperor, a Titan. Even that did not save you. Do not rely on anyone but yourself. Do not avoid anyone's eyes. You've done nothing to be ashamed of, and it is not you who should be looking away. If it's easier, become stone for the day. When he sees you, meet his gaze cold as the ice you know his heart is. Do not call him Sky Father. Do not bow to him. Do not look away, he doesn't deserve that luxury. When he says your name, refuse to look like prey. Instead, hold your head up high and let him see the blade you hide in your eyes. So what if he is a God. So what if he is a God. So what if he is even King of all the Gods. Do not let him forget he was wrong.

# Ariadne

If they tell you of a girl, full of mourning
and family secrets, a princess with
a terrible heritage, allow me to change that
to a slightly different perspective of more
than a woman who had a monster for a brother.
I was born Helios and Zeus's granddaughter,
but dance and balance were in my blood.
This is why I gave Theseus the way to murder
my own blood. I sent Asterion the compassion
he needed in the form of an ending to his suffering,
and named the labyrinth for what it was,
a cage and a mass grave.

When Theseus left me I was not surprised;
he did not want a girl who could draw blood
in brutal ways, for remorselessness is only seen
as pretty on men. He was too mortal for me
anyway, and I have spent too much time
in the company of darkness to become
wholesome when my quiet comes
from the corners of a labyrinth that
holds the bones of many heroes like him.
Dionysus found me soon after,
and loved every quiet darkness in me.
This is why I gave him my heart willingly,
for I found him a worthier lover.
After all, why should I settle for human
when I could have my own wild God?

# Aftermath

# Atlas, in Our Era

The star had not, contrary to popular opinion, lost her way. No, she knew exactly what she was doing. She had fallen on purpose, much to the shock of her siblings and her parents and her ancestors. No one in her constellation had ever decided to take such a drastic step. But she had always been a strange little star, glowing in the rightmost corner of this forgotten constellation, and she was not content. From when she was conceived as nebulae, she had been trouble and her parents knew it, even crafting the molecular structure.

In a way, no one was surprised when she fell. Yet at once, everyone was surprised when she fell. Cascading through the galaxy, burning brighter than ever before, the star finally met her destination. A two thousand five hundred foot-wide mountain range on a small, sapphire planet. As she landed – a shuddering going through the planet, a deep, sepia stardust-filled crater widening under the impact – she changed herself into the spiritless molecular form all stars take when they meet where they are about to fall.

'Hello.' She spoke softly and clearly to the mountains. At first, there was nothing. No response. The mountains looked cold, laden with a dappled blanket of fog. A gloom radiated from them, and for a long time the star just waited. Just as she was about to give up, a voice resonated from the depths of the fog.

'Hello' – the fog trembled as the rumble shook through all two thousand five hundred feet of the mountain. 'Why are you here?'

'To see you,' said the formless shape that was once a nebula. 'Why do you still hold up the cosmos, Titan? The era of the Gods has passed. Zeus has closed his doors on the earth forever. Man no longer needs the Gods and Gods no longer need man.'

A quaking, then a shape began to form in the side of the mountain. A face, large, older than anything anyone could have ever dreamt, somewhere between the face of a giant and a God spoke: 'I know this. You tell me nothing new.'

'You have freedom now to leave. Nothing stops you from doing so,' continued the star, as though she had never been interrupted.

Atlas was silent. 'And where would I go?'

'Home.'

The Titan released a sound from his mountain-made mouth which was almost a laugh and it made the planet shake. 'This *is* home for me.'

The star was surprised. She had fallen all this way to tell Atlas that he was finally free but the Titan didn't seem to want to budge. Instead, he continued to hold the weight of the cosmos. As the star looked up, she saw all of her family twinkling at her worriedly and dangerously.

There was a myth that each star passed to their child once they were born, and that was the myth of a Titan, on a sapphire blue planet, holding the cosmos up so they didn't fall. That he had kneeled for ages, long after the Gods who made it so were gone. The stars, the planets, the galaxies lived in fear that one day the Titan would learn what had come to pass and finally leave his post. And they all kept wishing no one ever told this Titan so.

This had struck the little star as grossly unjust and she had thought that this, if anything, was a good reason to fall. Someone had to tell the Titan that he was free. After all, a universe held up by a force kept captive defeated the entire purpose of its existing from its own free will. A paradox of the highest proportions.

But here, the star had found that the Titan ... had always known.

'I am the father of gardens and gardeners. I cannot leave, or who will tend to the graveyards of the stars?' asked Atlas gently.

'They'll be fine,' said the star glaring up at her family who twinkled nervously in response.

Atlas was silent. 'Have they ever told you that love is the oldest form of conservation and preservation? When I was a young Titan, I tended my gardens for eons, watched Gods fall and heroes die in a second to claim what was in them. A garden is an invention of patience. Of effort, and of pain and of endlessness.'

'So you won't leave then?' asked the star, slowly beginning to understand.

'No. Never. I still have the largest garden of all to maintain.'

'But ... there is no one to stop you, did you not hear me? All the old Gods are dead! Zeus cannot force his old rules upon you.'

'If I leave, the cosmos will descend into chaos.'

'But, that's not your problem.'

'It is.'

'Why?'

'For this is my nature, child.' Atlas smiled, unexpectedly tender on such a large face turned to stone. 'My mother nearly named me Pistis.'

'What does that mean?'

'It means loyal one.'

# A Glossary

**Achilles:** Greek hero warrior of Troy. His Goddess mother Thetis (a Nereid, water nymph) dipped him in the river Styx to give him invulnerability but had to hold him by one of his heels, thus making it his only weak spot. Lover of Patroclus.

**Aether:** Personification of the upper sky and light. Son of primordials Nyx (Night) and Erebus (Darkness) and brother of Hemera (Day).

**Agamemnon:** King of Mycene and Commander of the united Greek forces who fought the battle of Troy. Father of Iphigenia.

**Amphitrite:** Sea Goddess and wife of Poseidon; also an older Goddess of Titan blood because she is an Oceanid (daughter of Oceanus and Tethys).

**Andromeda:** Daughter of Ethiopian king Cepheus and queen Cassiopeia. Cassiopeia's hubris about Andromeda's beauty drew the ire of the Gods and Poseidon demanded the sacrifice of Andromeda to a sea monster as restitution for the insult.

**Apate:** Personification of deceit. Daughter of Nyx (the night).

**Aphrodite:** Goddess of Love, Beauty and Passion. Born of the castration of Ouranos and sea foam. One of the Twelve Olympians.

**Apollo:** God of the Sun, Music and Healing, son of Zeus and Leto (Titan Goddess of motherhood) and twin brother of Artemis (Goddess of the Hunt). One of the Twelve Olympians.

**Ares:** God of War. Son of Hera and Zeus. One of the Twelve Olympians.

**Argos:** Faithful dog of Odysseus. Left in Ithaca, when Odysseus returned Argos was very old and close to death. Unfortunately, as Odysseus could not risk being recognised, he could not give Argos a pat and say goodbye.

**Ariadne:** Daughter of King Minos and Queen Pasiphae of Crete, she helped Theseus escape the Labyrinth after he killed the Minotaur. She was left by Theseus on the shores of Naxos where the God Dionysus discovered and then wed her.

**Aristaeus:** God of Rural Arts and Practices – bee-keeping, animal husbandry, herbalism. Son of Apollo and Cyrene (Queen and ruler of the city of Cyrene).

**Artemis:** Goddess of the Moon, the Wild and the Hunt. Daughter of Zeus and Leto, and twin sister of Apollo. One of the Twelve Olympians.

**Asclepius:** God of Medicine. Son of Apollo with Coronis (Thelessian princess who went on to become the constellation Corvus). The rod of Asclepius is a symbol of medicine to this day.

**Asteria:** Titan Goddess of Nocturnal Oracles and Falling Stars. Mother of Hecate and wife to Perseus, Titan God of Destruction.

**Asterion:** The Minotaur, a bull-headed monster that lived in the Labyrinth at Crete.

**Athena:** Goddess of Wisdom and Warfare. Patron of Athens. Daughter of Zeus and Metis (Titan Goddess of Cunning). One of the Twelve Olympians.

**Atlas:** A Titan condemned to hold the heavens on his shoulders for all eternity. He was the son of one of the original Titans, Iapetus, and Oceanid Asia.

**Atropos:** One of the Three Fates, also known as the Moirai. She was the one who decided the end of mortals' lives by cutting their threads with her shears.

**Briseis:** Princess of Lyrnessus, a city allied with Troy. She was captured by Achilles when he burned down her city and killed her family and that of her husband.

**Brontes:** A giant with one eye, one of the three original Cyclopes – all blacksmiths that worked in Haephestus's volcano.

**Calliope:** Chief of the Nine Muses, Muse of Epic Poetry. Daughter of Zeus and Mnemosyne (Memory personified).

**Cerberus:** Hound of Hades who had three heads and a serpent's tail. He was the guardian of the gates of the Underworld who prevented the dead from leaving and the living from entering.

**Cetus:** Sea monster sent by Poseidon to devour Andromeda.

**Charybdis:** Originally a nymph who was the daughter of Poseidon, and helped him with his feud against Zeus. Zeus cursed her by turning her into a monster with an unquenchable thirst for the sea. She and Scylla made a treacherous strait together.

**Circe:** Goddess of Magic and Witch of Aeaea. Daughter of the Titan Sun God Helios. She turned men who visited her island into pigs.

**Clotho:** One of the Three Fates or Moriai. She spun the thread of human life.

**Cyclopes (*pl.*):** Children of Ouranos and Gaia. Along with the Hecatoncheires, they were thrown into Tartarus by their father because of how they looked.

**Danaë:** Mother of Perseus. Zeus impregnated her by becoming golden rain that fell on her through the cracks of her ceiling. Her father had hoped to keep her childless because of the prophecy that he would be killed by his daughter's son. He tossed her and the baby in a box into the sea to be rid of them.

**Delphin:** God of the Dolphin, he became a constellation because he helped to convince Amphitrite to be Poseidon's bride.

**Demeter:** Goddess of the Harvest, Growth and Fertility of the Earth, mother of Persephone. One of the Twelve Olympians.

**Dionysus:** God of Wine, Hedonism and Madness. Husband of Ariadne. Dionysus is twice born – once of his mortal mother Semele who was killed and then of Zeus, who brought the baby to full term by placing him in his thigh. One of the Twelve Olympians.

**Doris:** One of the Oceanids and wife to Nereus, mother of the fifty Nereids.

**Echidna:** Mother of Monsters, half woman, half snake, and wife to Typhon. Several of the most famous monsters were her children, including Cerberus, Hydra, Sphinx, Chimera and the Caucasian Eagle.

**Eos:** The Goddess of Dawn, sister to Helios and Selene (the moon). Daughter of Hyperion.

**Erebus:** The primordial personification of the darkness. Consort of Nyx, and child of Khaos.

**the Erinyes (*pl.*):** Chthonic Goddesses of Vengeance and Justice, and punishers of Gods and mortals alike who break oaths, swear false oaths and betray.

**Europa:** Mother of Minos, Rhadamanthus and Sarpedon, and one of the victims of Zeus. He abducted her in the form of a bull.

**Eurydice:** Oak nymph and a wife to Orpheus (musician son of Apollo), who loved her so dearly he travelled to the Underworld to bring her back. Unfortunately, Orpheus failed and her soul returned to the Underworld.

**Eurynome:** Pre-Olympian queen and the mother of all things according to at least one Pelasgian myth.

**Gaia (*also* Gaea):** Personification of the Earth and first daughter of Khaos.

**Gorgon:** mythical monstresses, most famously remembered as the mortal who was cursed to become a monster, Medusa, and the two immortal Gorgon sisters, Stheno and Euryale.

**Hades:** God of the Underworld and brother to Zeus and Poseidon.

**Hecate:** Goddess of Necromancy, she was raised in the underworld after the death of her mother Asteria.

**Hecatoncheires:** The three hundred-handed, fifty-headed children of Gaia and Ouranos. Ouranos cast them into Tartarus. According to some myths, they made him so uncomfortable he pushed them back into Gaia's womb.

**Hecuba:** Wife of Priam and Queen of Troy, mother to Paris, Hector and seventeen other princes and princesses of Troy.

**Helen:** Queen of Sparta and daughter of Zeus who ran away with Paris, leaving her husband Menelaus. Hers is the face that set sail a thousand ships.

**Helios:** God of the Sun. Son of Hyperion and brother to Eos and Selene.

**Hemera:** Primordial personification of the day. Daughter of Nyx and Erebus.

**Hephaestus:** God of Blacksmiths, Volcanoes and Fire. Son of Hera and one of the Twelve Olympians.

**Hera:** Goddess of Marriage and Childbirth and the Queen of the Gods. Wife of Zeus.

**Heracles:** Hero of Greece, and son of Zeus and Alcmene. He murdered his wife and children in a fit of madness and was given twelve tasks to redeem himself.

**Hermes:** God of Trade, Trickery and Heraldry. Son of Zeus and Maia, one of the Pleiades. He was also the messenger of the Olympians and played a significant role during the Titanomachy. He is one of the Twelve Olympians.

**Hestia:** Virgin Goddess of Hearth, Architecture, Home and Family. Hestia used to be one of the Olympians, but vacated her spot on the council to live among mortals. The vacancy was filled by Dionysus.

**Hippolyta:** Amazon queen and daughter to Ares. Her tribe was slaughtered by Heracles and his men on his twelve tasks.

**Hyperion:** Titan God of Light, son of Ouranos and Gaia, and one of the original Twelve Titans.

**Icarus:** Son of Daedalus, the greatest craftsman on earth and creator of the Labyrinth. Daedalus and Icarus were prisoners of Minos on the island of Crete, and Daedalus crafted wings for them both of feathers and wax. His warning to Icarus was not to fly too close to the sun as it would melt his wings. Icarus ignored the advice and fell into the sea and drowned.

**Io:** Nymph and ancestor to many heroes. One of Zeus's first victims. He abducted her and turned her into a cow so no one would recognise her and her family would not find her.

**Iphigenia:** Daughter of Agamemnon who was sacrificed by her father so that the Greeks' ships could sail to Troy. In most versions of the myth, the Goddess Artemis sees the courage in this girl and takes her away to be a high priestess.

**Keres:** Death spirits who personified violent death. Daughters of Nyx and Chthonic deities. They are considered similar to the Valkyries of ancient Norse mythology.

**Khaos:** The chasm from which the universe was born. The mother of all the primordials and the Greek creation myth.

**Kore:** The girlhood name of Persephone when she was the Goddess of Spring and not yet the Queen of Hell.

**Kraken:** A Norse name for Cetus, the sea monster.

**Kronos:** Father of the Olympians who was King of the Titans and the heavens before his son Zeus defeated him.

**Lachesis:** One of the Three Fates or the Moirai. Measurer of the thread of destiny.

**Lamia:** a revered princess and a lover to Zeus. Hera punished her for her liaisons with Zeus by giving her a madness which made her kill her children, after which she became a widely mocked hermit. Zeus turned her into a monster so that those who mocked her would fear her.

**Leto:** Goddess of Motherhood and sister to Asteria. Mother of Apollo and Artemis.

**Medusa:** Originally a beautiful high priestess of the Temple of Athena. A victim of Poseidon's lust, she prayed to Athena for help and the Goddess turned her into a monster with snakes for hair and the capacity to turn anyone into stone.

**Megara:** Wife of Heracles. He murdered her along with their children in a fit of rage.

**Menelaus:** King of Sparta and husband of Helen of Troy. He was also brother to Agamemnon.

**Metis:** Oceanid, Goddess of Cunning and first wife of Zeus. She also raised Zeus in secret and taught him everything he knew. He devoured her because it was prophesied that she would give birth to a son who would overthrow him. Mother of Athena.

**Mnemosyne:** One of the original Twelve Titans. The personification of memory and mother to the Nine Muses.

**Mormolykeia (*pl.*):** Literally translated, it means the hideous ones; a fable used to frighten children.

**the Nemean lion:** A vicious monster who lived in Nemea. Killed by Heracles during one of his twelve tasks.

**the Nereids:** The fifty daughters of Nereus and Doris, the Nereids were water nymphs who were helpful to sailors.

**Nyx:** Personification of the night and one of the first primordials. Daughter of Chaos and mother to many primordial Gods and Goddesses.

**the Oceanids (*pl.*):** The three thousand River Goddesses who were children of Oceanus and Tethys, two of the original Twelve Titan children.

**Odysseus:** King of Ithaca and a grandson of Hermes. One of the commanders in the battle of Troy, Odysseus was known for his cunning.

**Oizys:** Goddess of Misery, Grief, Anxiety and Depression. Daughter of Nyx.

**Ouranos:** The mate Gaia crafted for herself and the personification of the sky. He was the father of Gaia's Titan children and the Hecatoncheires and Cyclopes. He was overthrown by his youngest Titan son, Kronos.

**Pallas:** Warrior daughter of Triton, Sea God. Lover and best friend of Athena. She met her end under Athena's spear amid friendly combat; Zeus distracted her with the Aegis so she misstepped. Athena, in remembrance, placed her name before her own and called herself Pallas Athena from then on.

**Paris:** Prince of Troy who brought about its fall by eloping with Helen, the Queen of Sparta. Paris is known for his role in choosing Aphrodite when the three Goddesses – Hera, Athena and Aphrodite – asked him to give the apple of discord to the Goddess he found most beautiful. Athena and Hera cursed him.

**Patroclus:** Warrior at Troy and lover of Achilles. When Patroclus died at the hands of Hector, Achilles nearly single-handedly destroyed Troy.

**Peitho:** Goddess of Persuasion and Seduction, and wife of Hermes. She was also a companion of Aphrodite.

**Penelope:** Queen of Ithaca who ruled with shrewd common sense while her husband Odysseus fought the war for the Greeks in Troy.

**Persephone:** Queen of the Underworld and daughter of Demeter, who became wife of Hades. Her name means the Destroyer.

**Perseus:** Husband to Andromeda and founder of Mycene. He beheaded Medusa.

**Phaeton:** Originally the son of Helios, in this book, the son of Apollo. He thought he could drive the sun chariot to impress his friends but slipped and went off course and ended up setting half the world on fire. Zeus killed him with a lightning bolt to prevent more damage.

**Phoebe:** One of the original Twelve Titans and Goddess of Shining. Her name is the reason behind Artemis and Apollo sometimes being called Phoebus Apollo and Phoebe Artemis.

**Pirithous:** King of the Lapiths of Larissa. He and Theseus pledged to carry off daughters of Zeus and they descended into the Underworld to steal Persephone for Pirithous. Persephone punished his insolence by setting the Erinyes on them. In some versions of the tale, she invites Theseus and Pirithous to sit at her table to eat, but the chairs turn into bonds that leave the two men trapped till Heracles was able to free Theseus (but not Pirithous).

**Polydorus:** Youngest son of Priam and Hecuba, and a prince of Troy. He was sent with gold to Thrace under the protection of King Polymestor. When Troy fell, the king murdered Polydorus by drowning him.

**Polymestor:** King of Thrace who betrayed the oath of Priam by killing his son. When Hecuba found out, she killed Polymestor's sons and blinded him.

**Poseidon:** God of the Sea and one of the Twelve Olympians. Son of Rhea and Kronos.

**Priam:** King of Troy and father of Hector, Paris, Cassandra, among others.

**Prometheus:** Titan, father of man and best friend of Zeus who crafted mortals from clay. Prometheus had the gift of prophecy and was punished for giving man divine fire.

**Rhea:** Mother of the Olympians and one of the original Twelve Titans. Wife of Kronos who helped to defeat him.

**Scylla:** Legendary monster who features in the Odyssey.

**Selene:** Titan Goddess of the Moon, sister to Helios and Eos, and daughter of Hyperion.

**Semele:** mortal daughter of Cadmus and Harmonia (daughter of Ares and Aphrodite), who became mother to Dionysus by Zeus. Unfortunately she was tricked by Hera into asking Zeus to appear to her in his true form, which then incinerated her while Dionysus was still in her womb. Zeus rescued Dionysus by sewing him into his thigh. When he grew up Dionysus rescued his mother from Hades.

**Tethys:** One of the original Twelve Titans and mother to thousands of Oceanids and River Gods. Wife to Oceanus. Daughter to Gaia and Ouranos.

**Theia:** One of the original Twelve Titans and mother to Helios, Selene and Eos. Consort of Hyperion.

**Themis:** Personification of divine order and fairness, justice and law. She is one of the original Twelve Titans.

**Theseus:** Hero who defeated the Minotaur of Crete.

**Titanides (*pl.*):** The six original Titan Goddesses.

**the Titanomachy:** The ten thousand-year war between the Titans and the Olympians started by Zeus and Kronos. The Titans lost and were sent to Tartarus, the innermost circle of hell reserved for immortals.

**Triton:** Son of Poseidon and Amphitrite, and father to Pallas, who was Athena's lover and comrade. Triton raised Athena as his own and taught her the wisdom of warfare when Zeus couldn't raise her himself.

**Typhon:** Husband to Echidna and the son of Tartarus and Gaia, created by Gaia to defeat the Olympians.

**Zeus:** The first Olympian and King of the Gods. He also defeated his father Kronos to gain access to the throne of the Heavens by starting the Titanomachy.

# Acknowledgements

**With thanks to:**

My parents, for raising me with mythology in my bones.

My grandparents, for every old clothbound book of mythology that sits in their homes.

My brother, for being reassuring and reading the stories with me.

Emma, for always believing in me and being the most incredible editor a writer could ask for.

Niki, for being the loveliest and best agent, and my champion.

Steve, for being my rock, always.

Tristan and Joanna, for being the dearest of friends and always believing in me.

Clare and Layla, my very best friend and my lovely niece.

Amanda and Trista, my found family.

Nikesh, for being an absolute inspiration.

The team over at Ebury, especially Chloe, Stephenie and Michelle for being marvellous and supporting me throughout this process.

Shaun, Alison, Rebekah, Dave, Clara, Lauz, Emma, Heather, Ross, Matt, for their friendship, kindness and support while writing – especially when I thought I would fail.

Henry and Tom, for their motivation during this book's creation and my next venture.

Robert Graves, Homer, Apollodorus, Hesiod, Ovid, Margaret Atwood, Madeline Miller, Edith Hamilton and Stephen Fry for writing the most excellent books which aided me along the way.

And finally and always, to you who found this book and joined me on this journey from the heavens to the underworld to meet monsters, Gods, Goddesses and mortals. I hope this book brings you the belief that you are a divine hero too.